ALBUM OF
AMERICAN HISTORY

RELATED WORKS

Atlas of American History

Dictionary of American History

Dictionary of American Biography

ALBUM OF AMERICAN HISTORY

VOLUME IV
END OF AN ERA

James Truslow Adams
Editor in Chief

R. V. Coleman
Managing Editor

Joseph G. E. Hopkins
Associate Editor

Atkinson Dymock
Art Director

NEW YORK
CHARLES SCRIBNER'S SONS

ITH this fourth volume we complete the *Album of American History* as originally planned. That plan was to tell, primarily by means of *pictures*, the story of the United States from 1492 to 1917. Throughout the whole series the editors, although hoping for pictorial effectiveness, have endeavored first to present a truthful graphic record of events. Every picture has been scrupulously authenticated and documented. We have travelled a long road from the first lasting impact of European civilization on America in the fifteenth century down to the colossal refluent wave of American influence on Europe at the time of our entry into World War I. The centuries covered were marked by constant change with accelerating rapidity of tempo.

In this fourth and final volume we see William Jennings Bryan, Theodore Roosevelt and Woodrow Wilson in action. We watch the development of the automobile and radio. We observe the gradual mechanization of farm and home. The flight of heavier-than-air planes becomes a reality. Looking through the pages of pictures, with their explanatory and accurate thread of text, the younger readers of the earlier volumes will realize the difference between the new world of this volume and *their* own known world; while older readers will relive the exciting changes of their youth.

One is inclined to ask of the latter group whether they were conscious when they saw these changes beginning, of what their implications would some day mean? Did they consider how man as an individual was shrinking while his adaptations of steam and electric power were giving him strength beyond all prior reckoning? As they look at the pictures of the last great "openings" of the Public Domain can they recall that they gave a thought, at the time when those incidents occurred, to the fact that they were witnessing the beginning of vast changes in the social, political and economic concepts of Americans? Now, as those of a new generation look at the pictures which show early gas-engine tractors; dim, flickering movies; antiquated "horseless carriages," they may comprehend better, perhaps than we older ones who actually saw all these beginnings, what they were to mean in transforming the America of the previous three volumes. And the younger readers also may realize, better than they have heretofore, that the daily world of things which they take as much for granted as a part of nature, as they do the sun, the air and the rain, are things only of yesterday, many of them first thought of or made in the days when their fathers were of their own age; the products not of a permanent and enduring universe but of a highly complex and unstable type of man's civilization, which could all too easily break down.

In the era covered by this volume, tangible things came from ideas but ideas also were important in initiating intangible things in the form of movements which also played their part in the rapid march of change. Reform was the word as the new century opened; political reform, urged on by the often raucous voices of muck-raking journalists; social reform, dinned into American ears by militant and professional social workers; suffrage for women; prohibition; anti-militarism! We sense the power of these forces from pictures of the effects they caused. The people of the United States were on the whole looking forward to a world which would become progressively more controlled, tidier, with our scientific discoveries lending themselves to a fuller and happier life for all men. The disillusion began with the First World War, and this concluding volume ends with pictures of American troops moving into battle in a European conflict which was to conclude a long era and to divide the stream of history into what had been and the unknown of what may lie ahead.

As we finish our task it is a pleasure to render thanks to all those who have given this project their generous and valuable aid.

In the making of this volume, as in the case of the previous ones, the museums, libraries, business corporations, and public institutions of the country have contributed freely from their pictorial collections and helped us with advice. Due to the fact that in the period covered we have been working within that of amateur photography we are even more indebted than before to individuals who contributed cherished snapshots which portray vividly the life of the time. To all who have helped, and whose assistance is not otherwise more specifically acknowledged, the editors express their gratitude.

As Editor in Chief it is with both regret and deep appreciation of all that they have done that I give my Hail and Farewell to my associates. There have been some changes in the staff during the years the work has been in progress but to all, those who have been with it from the start and to those who have passed on to other things and been already thanked in previous volumes, I wish again to say how truly grateful I am for their teamwork, knowledge, skill and all the rest they have contributed to make my original idea of such a book take the form it has and without whom it could not possibly have been done.

I have now worked with the Managing Editor, Mr. R. V. Coleman, over nine years—on the six volumes of the *Dictionary of American History,* the

Atlas of American History, and the four volumes of this *Album*. It is difficult to say, for the eleventh time, much that is new as to my always expressed appreciation of his invaluable aid. But now, as I said above, that it must be *Ave atque Vale*, I do want to reiterate that I owe him an unpayable debt for his help in all these eleven volumes, and I shall always retain my admiration for his knowledge not only of American history but also of historians, institutions and of the administration of such works as we have been jointly engaged upon.

The Associate Editor of this volume, Mr. Joseph G. E. Hopkins, has had charge of the difficult task of arranging the pictures and of writing the running text, a far more difficult one than most who skim these pages can realize.

Preliminary to the fine work done by Mr. Hopkins was that of Mary Wells McNeill, whose wide-flung task was to secure the pictorial material and to put it into usable form.

Preliminary to that, again, was the work of Ethel M. Watson, who has done with great ability the patient and knowledgeable research necessary to locate and secure the pictures.

Mr. Atkinson Dymock has had general supervision of the production of the book and has done a fine job under difficult circumstances.

Mr. William F. Koch has had charge of what we call the detailed "layout" of the volume, and to him and all the others I offer my deeply appreciative thanks.

And so, Farewell again, and may the future treat you well!

JAMES TRUSLOW ADAMS

June 25, 1948

ACKNOWLEDGMENT

IN THIS as in the previous volumes the editors have been assisted by the advice and co-operation of museums, libraries and individuals throughout the country. In general, proper credit has been given in the case of each picture reproduced but particular acknowledgment for especial help is due the following:

Aluminum Company of America, Pittsburgh, Pa.
American Car and Foundry Company, New York City
American Telephone and Telegraph Company, New York City
Anaconda Copper Mining Company, New York City
Mr. and Mrs. Walter C. Arensberg, Hollywood, Calif.
Atlanta University, Atlanta, Ga.
Mr. F. Ivor D. Avellino, The New York Public Library, New York City
N. W. Ayer & Son, Inc., Philadelphia, Pa.
The Municipal Museum of the City of Baltimore, Baltimore, Md.
The Best Foods, Inc., New York City
Bethlehem Steel Company, New York City
Bland Gallery, New York City
Byron Collection, Museum of the City of New York
California Historical Society, San Francisco, Calif.
Mr. Arthur Carlson, Curator of Prints, The New-York Historical Society, New York City
J. I. Case Company, Racine, Wis.
Mrs. Ralph Catterall, Curator of Prints and Manuscripts, The Valentine Museum, Richmond, Va.
Chicago, Burlington & Quincy Railroad Company, Chicago, Ill.
Chicago Lawn Historical Society and Chicago Public Library, Ill.
The Corcoran Gallery of Art, Washington, D. C.
Mr. Christopher Crittenden, Director, North Carolina State Department of Archives and History, Raleigh, N. C.

Mr. Thomas B. Dancey, Dearborn, Mich.

The J. Clarence Davies Collection, Museum of the City of New York

Dearborn Historical Commission, Dearborn, Mich.

Detroit Institute of Arts, Detroit, Mich.

Detroit Public Library, Detroit, Mich.

Miss Marjory Douglas, Curator, Missouri Historical Society, St. Louis, Mo.

The Edison Institute, Dearborn, Mich.

Enoch Pratt Free Library, Baltimore, Md.

Mrs. Irene Castle Enzinger, Lake Forest, Ill.

The Essex Institute, Salem, Mass.

Mrs. Frank Ewing, Grand Rapids, Mich.

Florida East Coast Railway Company, St. Augustine, Fla.

Ford Motor Company, Dearborn, Mich.

Robert Fridenberg Galleries, New York City

General Electric Company, Schenectady, N. Y.

General Motors Corporation, New York City

Mrs. Bert Gilmor, Los Angeles, Calif.

Grace Line, New York City

The Great Atlantic and Pacific Tea Company, New York City

Great Northern Railway Company, St. Paul, Minn.

H. J. Heinz Company, Pittsburgh, Pa.

The Hempstead Library, Hempstead, N. Y.

Mr. Myron F. Henkel, Springfield, Ill.

J. E. Henry Collection, Enoch Pratt Free Library, Baltimore, Md.

The Home Insurance Company, New York City

The Indiana Historical Society, Indianapolis, Ind.

International Harvester Company, Chicago, Ill.

Iowa State Department of History and Archives, Des Moines, Iowa

The Johns Hopkins University, Baltimore, Md.

Johns-Manville Corporation, New York City

Johnson & Johnson, New Brunswick, N. J.

Kansas State Historical Society, Topeka, Kans.

Mr. Joseph Katz, Baltimore, Md.

Mr. Charles B. King, Larchmont, N. Y.

Bella C. Landauer Collection at The New-York Historical Society, New York City

Lick Observatory, Mount Hamilton, Calif.

Robinson Locke Collection, The New York Public Library, New York City

The Long Island Railroad, New York City

Mrs. Ruth Locker MacDonald, Two Harbors, Minn.

Mack-International Motor Truck Corporation, New York City

Miss Grace Mayer, Curator of Prints, Museum of the City of New York
Metropolitan Museum of Art, New York City
Minnesota Historical Society, St. Paul, Minn.
Missouri Historical Society, St. Louis, Mo.
Film Library, The Museum of Modern Art, New York City
The National Archives, Washington, D. C.
National Park Service
National Woman's Christian Temperance Union, Evanston, Ill.
Nebraska State Historical Society, Lincoln, Neb.
Public Relations Office, University of Nebraska, Lincoln, Neb.
Nevada State Historical Society, Reno, Nev.
Board of Commissioners of the Port of New Orleans, New Orleans, La.
Board of Transportation of The City of New York
The New York Curb Exchange, New York City
The New-York Historical Society, New York City
Museum of the City of New York
The New York Public Library, New York City
Mr. Stephen L. Newnham, Philadelphia, Pa.
North Carolina State Department of Archives and History, Raleigh, N. C.
Otis Elevator Company, New York City
Phillips Memorial Gallery, Washington, D. C.
The University of Pittsburgh, Pittsburgh, Pa.
Pomona Public Library, Pomona, Calif.
Princeton University Library, Princeton, N. J.
Public Roads Administration, Washington, D. C.
Purdue University, Lafayette, Ind.
Radio Corporation of America, New York City
Ravenswood-Lake View Historical Association, sponsored by The Chicago
        Public Library, Chicago, Ill.
Jacob A. Riis Collection, Museum of the City of New York
Rockefeller Foundation, New York City
Roosevelt Memorial Association, New York City
St. Louis County Historical Society, Duluth, Minn.
Captain Fred A. Samuelson, Ludington, Mich.
San Mateo County Historical Association, San Mateo, Calif.
Sears, Roebuck and Co., Chicago, Ill.
The Alfred E. Smith Collection, Museum of the City of New York
Smith College Archives, Northampton, Mass.
Smithsonian Institution, Washington, D. C.
Sperry Gyroscope Company, Inc., Great Neck, N. Y.
Standard Oil Company of Ohio, Cleveland, Ohio

Dr. Robert Taft, University of Kansas, Lawrence, Kans.

The Library of the University of Texas, Austin, Tex.

Tuskegee Institute, Tuskegee Institute, Ala.

United States Navy Department, Washington, D. C.

United States Signal Corps, Washington, D. C.

United States Steel Corporation, New York City

Mr. R. W. G. Vail, Director, The New-York Historical Society, New York City

The Valentine Museum, Richmond, Va.

Charles van Ravenswaay Collection, Missouri Historical Society, St. Louis, Mo.

Mr. Sylvester L. Vigilante, The New York Public Library, New York City

The Waldorf-Astoria, New York City

Waukesha County Historical Society, Waukesha, Wis.

Western Electric Company, New York City

Westinghouse Electric Corporation, Pittsburgh, Pa.

Miss Jeanne Elizabeth Wier, Nevada State Historical Society, Reno, Nev.

Wisconsin State Historical Society, Madison, Wis.

Wyoming State Library and State Historical Department, Cheyenne, Wyo.

CONTENTS

1

THE NINETIES WERE NOT SO GAY

"It was the best of times; it was the worst of times"—as always. The carefree young of 1893, for whom father did the worrying, may be forgiven for thinking their time a golden age.

While the newly elected President Cleveland pondered in dismay the problems of an empty treasury, his joyful supporters made the most of their election bets.

Courtesy, Bland Gallery, New York City

The ominous "blue-ticket" appeared in many a pay envelope. When the men started home from their day's work, they couldn't be sure that the stacks of the mill would still be smoking in a week's time. Abroad in the nation were uncertain hope, incomplete faith, and the prospect of charity. And, suddenly, there was financial panic.

Courtesy, Mr. Joseph Katz, Baltimore, Md.

Hard Times

Henry Vincent, *The Story of the Commonweal.* 1894
Courtesy, W. B. Conkey Company, Hammond, Ind.

All across the land were symbols of the calamity like the one shown *above*. Nor was industry the sole casualty of '93. Hard times closed in like an early winter on financial institutions and railroads. Mortgage holders howled for their money. "Out of work" men lounged restlessly about the house or gathered in the corner saloons to talk and grumble; their wives fretted and grew sharp-tongued with anxiety.

Courtesy, The Franklin Society,
New York City

The thrifty ones shook coins out of house savings banks as shown *above*.

People in the cities grew used to the sight of "bread-lines."

Courtesy, Scribner Art File

Calamity-Howlers

Driven into politics by poor credit status, falling farm prices and the throttling hand of the railroads on their economic gullets, the farmers of the Mid-West flocked into the "People's Party," or Populist Movement.

Mary Elizabeth Lease (*below*) urged her Kansas friends to raise "less corn and more hell."

Courtesy, Kansas State Historical Society, Topeka

Why the Farmer Owns the Farm
or "HEADS, I WIN; TAILS, HE LOSES."

A half century ago, when the wild Indian and the buffalo roamed at will across our western plains, and the coyotes howled their nightly chorus unafraid, this country was different from what it is now.

The "Homestead Act" was passed; an invitation to all citizens of the United States to go forth and settle the American wilderness, and make it blossom as the rose. This act did not affect all men alike, as results have plainly showed.

Courtesy, Wisconsin State Historical Society, Madison

Courtesy, Kansas State Historical Society, Topeka

In a struggle for control of the Kansas legislature, the Populists contested the election of thirteen Republican representatives, and on the failure of this move they seized possession of the legislative chamber. Ousted by the Republicans, they besieged the State House, and Governor Lewelling ordered the militia out to keep order, as shown *above*.

Armed groups of Republicans and Populists and special deputies assembled by the local Sheriff jostled against the militia and battle was imminent.

By a decision of the Kansas Supreme Court, the Republicans were declared properly seated and the Republican speaker duly elected. The peace was preserved thereafter in the legislative hall by the special sergeants-at-arms shown *right*.

Courtesy, Kansas State Historical Society, Topeka

Symptoms of Trouble

In the great centers of trade, closed exchanges were symptoms of the financial paralysis. Brokers gathered in an unwonted and uneasy quiet.

Courtesy, New York Coffee and Sugar Exchange, Inc., New York City

Chambers of Commerce met in session (*right*) to discuss ways and means of breaking the deadlock, but President Cleveland clung to the belief that tariff reduction and administrative reform were enough—that the depression would cure itself automatically.

William F. Leggett and Frederick J. Chipman, *The City of Duluth and Environs.* 1895
Courtesy, The New-York Historical Society, New York City

At ports of entry, hordes of immigrants presented themselves, hopeful and undismayed.

Harper's Weekly, Aug. 26, 1893
Courtesy, Harper & Brothers, New York City

Houses

The New England home was perennial. Changing modes in architecture left untouched the ancient austerity of Massachusetts and New Hampshire.

Joseph Dow, *History of the Town of Hampton, New Hampshire.* 1893
Courtesy, The New-York Historical Society, New York City

In the Middle West, "comfortable" people made a modest display of opulence in homes like the one shown *left*.

Courtesy, Iowa State Department of History and Archives, Des Moines

And in New York and Pennsylvania, the movement out of the cities into suburbs by those who could afford it set up a new pattern for living.

Harper's Bazar, Feb. 17, 1894
Courtesy, Harper's Bazaar, New York City

Interiors

Inside a late Victorian house, the evidences of financial competence were built-in and obvious. There was heavy grandeur in the entry hall and stair—

assurance of solid fare in the dining room appointments—

a self-conscious and formal elegance in the show place of the house—the parlor.

The People

Courtesy, Mr. Myron F. Henkel, Springfield, Ill.

The great majority of "comfortable" Americans lived in more homely style than that shown on page 6. In the picture *above*, the Judge plays solitaire after a day in court and his wife is reading by electric light in a typical "living-room."

The elderly lady from Michigan, to the *right*, would have had much to say about wasting money on a parlor, or time on card playing.

Courtesy, Mrs. Bert Gilmor, Los Angeles, Calif.

Their Children

Courtesy, Miss Dean McKoin, Monroe, La.

One of these children lived in Louisiana; the other in New York. They never met, but their expressions indicate a similarity of outlook on life—the result of a general, parental attitude.

Children were to be seen and not heard. They were to understand that life was an unvarying process of hard work, strict attention to duty, a gradual prosperity, a climax in "comfort," and a magisterial, independent old age. Children who did not observe this routine came inevitably to a bad end. Each family had its horrible example: Uncle Ben, who married an actress—Aunt Amy, whose husband drank (and she knew it when she married him).

Courtesy, Associate Editor

Shops

Before the chain-stores, the rise of
national advertising, and widespread distribution of packaged foods
established levels of quality that varied only slightly at more or less
standard prices, a grocer's knowledge
of his market was important. Retail-
ing was a very personal business, and
in the medium-sized American community your social condition could
be told by "where you traded."

Hardware stores stocked all kinds
of housekeeping goods as well as
plows, wagons and ten penny nails.

Just as a "lady" was judged
by her taste in clothes, so
a "gentleman" of the
Nineties could be assayed
by his taste in cigars. A
good cigar in the pocket
was a symbol of attain-
ment; its presentation to a
friend was ritualistic. And
in the words of the little
sign that hung in hundreds
of cigar stores:

   Cigarette smoke, like
      lighted punk,
   Hath a fetid stink, like
      a lively skunk.

All illustrations on this page are from William F. Leggett and Frederick J. Chipman, *The City of Duluth and Environs.* 1895. Courtesy, The New-York Historical Society, New York City

College

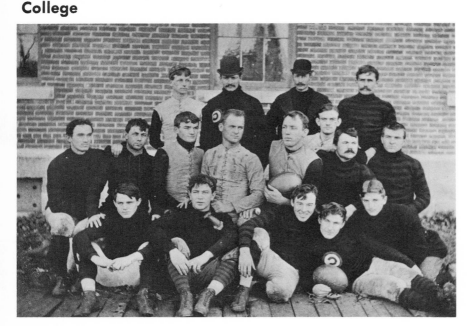

Courtesy, Purdue University, Lafayette, Ind.

Extremes met at American colleges in the Nineties. The boys and girls of the "comfortable" families were finding it socially important to attend the "U" along with boys and girls who were grimly working their way to a degree and a profession.

Football teams were deliberately rugged.

But there were boys and girls who read Swinburne and Oscar Wilde; who took their cue from the *Yellow Book*; who emulated the literary fashion in college "Lit" magazines and served (*right*) on their Editorial Boards.

Courtesy, Purdue University, Lafayette, Ind.

At the University of Nebraska, Chancellor Canfield was a pioneer in introducing gymnasium work and competitive athletics for the girl undergraduates. The dresses shown in the picture *left* were decried at the time as indecent.

Courtesy, Public Relations Office, University of Nebraska, Lincoln

Newspapers

Personal journalism was still a force in 1893. The country editor shown *right* had wide influence in his limited area. But the day of "features," syndicates and newspaper combines was coming and would push him to the wall.

Courtesy, Nebraska State Historical Society, Lincoln

William F. Leggett and Frederick J. Chipman, The City of Duluth and Environs. 1895 Courtesy, The New-York Historical Society, New York City

The *Duluth Press*, whose office is shown *left*, was owned by "Buffalo Bill" Cody and his sister. Every editorial department was staffed exclusively by women.

Through the street-level windows of the New York *Herald's* beautiful, new building on Herald Square, the passers-by could watch the wheels go round.

Harper's Weekly, Sept. 2, 1893. Courtesy, Harper & Brothers, New York City

Advertising drew to only a limited degree on art and literature for the propagation of its message. The *above* page is typical of the advertising of 1893.

All illustrations on this page are from *Harper's Weekly*, July 1, 1893, and Oct. 7, 1893 *Courtesy*, Harper & Brothers, New York City

Perils of Politics

Harper's Weekly, Nov. 18, 1893. *Courtesy*, Harper & Brothers, New York City

The scene *above* ensued when New York City reformers tried to serve a Supreme Court writ on John Y. McKane, boss of Gravesend and Coney Island. The writ required him to cease and desist from certain Election Day practices common to men in his political position. His answer, "This don't go here," and the riot that followed were talked of across the nation as examples of boss-rule arrogance.

At about the same date in Chicago a disappointed candidate for Corporation Counsel shot Mayor Carter Harrison.

Harper's Weekly, Nov. 11, 1893. *Courtesy*, Harper & Brothers, New York City

People in the News

Courtesy, The New York Public Library, New York City

Queen Liliuokalani of Hawaii protested that the "Republic of Hawaii" which had deposed her was a conspiracy of American interests against a friendly state, and President Cleveland agreed with her. But the provisional government refused to step down and the Queen remained deposed.

The Infanta Eulalia of Spain (*right*) stirred up a newspaper tempest during a visit to Chicago by her surprise at an "innkeeper's wife" pretending to social leadership.

Harper's Bazar, June 3, 1893
Courtesy, Harper's Bazaar, New York City

Hetty Green (*left*) was much in the news on the score of her fabulous wealth, her shrewd wit and her passion for litigation. A contemporary news account said she retained "enough counsellors to administer an empire."

Harper's Bazar, Oct. 19, 1895
Courtesy, Harper's Bazaar, New York City

Fashionable Folk

Dinner at Delmonico's (*right*) was a socially acceptable piece of ritual, though the older school still frowned on entertaining one's guests in a public place.

Entertaining in the home was the proper way—and the duller according to the rebellious younger married set.

Harper's Bazar, Dec. 7, 1895
Courtesy, Harper's Bazaar, New York City

Harper's Bazar, Feb. 11, 1893
Courtesy, Harper's Bazaar, New York City

Still firmly fixed in her social niche was the chaperone—the final arbiter (*right*). Nice, young people simply could not let themselves be talked about.

Harper's Bazar, Apr. 7, 1894
Courtesy, Harper's Bazaar, New York City

The Mode of 1893

The well-dressed woman looked to Paris for her styles as good Moslems looked to Mecca for their souls' salvation.

Harper's Bazar, Feb. 11, 1893
Courtesy, Harper's Bazaar, New York City

American magazines featured the latest creations of Worth, Doucet and Virot. For autumn and winter, the calling costume (*left*) and the evening gowns (*below*) were the height of the mode. The white satin gown in the center of the group was "bordered with a feather band around the skirt and richly trimmed with applied pearl passementerie. The draped bodice is taken into a deep girdle of passementerie, and the neck and short puffed sleeves are edged with feathers."

A hint of spring could be seen in the "novel, little bonnets" shown *below*.

Harper's Bazar, Apr. 8, 1893
Courtesy, Harper's Bazaar, New York City

Harper's Bazar, Feb. 4, 1893
Courtesy, Harper's Bazaar, New York City

The Mode of 1893 (Continued)

The ''Spring Maid'' decked herself in the artful simplicity shown
right, and sighed for the magnificence shown *below*.

Harper's Bazar, Feb. 25, 1893
Courtesy, Harper's Bazaar, New York City

Harper's Bazar, July 15, 1893
Courtesy, Harper's Bazaar, New York City

On the porches and lawns
of resort hotels from
Maine to California, the
daughters of America
wore the summer dresses
shown *right* and whiled
away the long, lazy days
with Mr. Howells' novels,
flirtation and *Harper's
Bazar*.

Harper's Bazar, May 13, 1893
Courtesy, Harper's Bazaar, New York City

Show Business

Courtesy, The New-York Historical Society, New York City

The "Road" was still an active and profitable branch of the American Theater. All around the country travelling shows advertised their arrival in small communities. In Montgomery, Ala. (*left*), the billboards of 1893 announced among other attractions the coming of Sousa's Band.

Below may be seen a typical "matinee" crowd leaving the theater.

Harper's Weekly, Apr. 28, 1894
Courtesy, Harper & Brothers, New York City

The Metropolitan Opera of New York offered the classic repertory to ladies and gentlemen who considered the efforts of the singers a harmonious accompaniment to their own conversation. After the performance, the box-holders finished their chat while awaiting their carriages in the private lobby shown *above*.

Harper's Weekly, Mar. 9, 1895
Courtesy, Harper & Brothers, New York City

The Dawn of "Realism"

In 1893, at the Boston Museum, James A. Herne's "Shore Acres" was produced precisely as he had written it—the first successful essay in realistic drama by an American playwright. Herne's "Drifting Apart" and "Margaret Fleming" had been too grim for the taste of the time.

Above is the famous "Kitchen Set" for the last act of "Shore Acres."

"Who 'teched them cranberries?" (Act II)

The brothers' quarrel in Act II.

Nathan'l and his niece (Act I)

American Art

The long bondage in which the "old" masters had held American patrons of art was coming to an end. It was found that we had produced a few masters of our own, but it took European recognition to advertise our artists in their own country.

The happy realism displayed in Eakins' painting of "Max Schmitt at the Single Sculls" (*left*) echoed in paint the hopefulness of Walt Whitman's message.

John Singer Sargent proved his technical skill and his eye for character in portraits like the one *below*.

The brooding genius of John LaFarge was widely praised, but the meaning of studies like the one shown *above* eluded the many.

American Art (*Continued*)

Americans were beginning to appreciate impressionism and mood in painting. In the painting *above*, Mary Cassatt expressed a typical grace and tenderness.

And by the Nineties, our connoisseurs had awakened to the fact that James Abbott McNeill Whistler was more than a clever phrasemaker and *poseur*. His paintings, like the study "Connie Gilchrist" (*above*), and etchings like the early "Black Lion Wharf" (*right*) came at last into their own.

Reform

Harper's Weekly, May 26, 1894
Courtesy, Harper & Brothers, New York City

Harper's Weekly, May 26, 1894
Courtesy, Harper & Brothers, New York City

Harper's Weekly, May 26, 1894
Courtesy, Harper & Brothers, New York City

The Reform School and the Chain Gang have become bywords for inhumanity, but in 1893 they were symptoms of enlightened approach to the problem of the criminal.

At Elmira Reformatory (as seen on this page), the inmates paraded to music, learned tinsmithing and woodturning, and attended lectures on literature.

Near Augusta, Ga., the Chain Gang (*right*) labored in the open air.

Courtesy, The New-York Historical Society, New York City

Temperance

The drive against the iniquities of the old-time saloon (*right*) intensified as the Woman's Christian Temperance Union grew strong under the guiding hand of Frances Willard (*below*). She wore herself out in the cause.

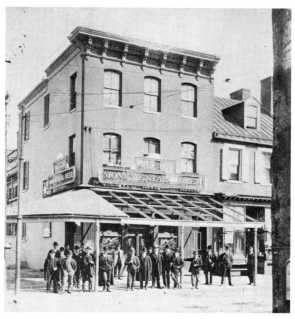

Courtesy, J. E. Henry Collection, Enoch Pratt Free Library, Baltimore, Md.

Miss Willard's study on the second floor of her home in Evanston, Ill., is shown *below*. The tall clock was made by one of her ancestors.

Courtesy, National Woman's Christian Temperance Union, Evanston, Ill.

Courtesy, National Woman's Christian Temperance Union, Evanston, Ill.

Fun

The dancers swayed under the arching boughs at an Indiana Harvest Jubilee, and there were always men and boys ready to climb the greasy pole at County Fairs.

Harper's Weekly, Sept. 30, 1893
Courtesy, Harper & Brothers, New York City

The more sedate, and the ailing, betook themselves to the quiet of spas like Bethesda Spring, Wis., shown *left*.

Courtesy, Waukesha County Historical Society, Waukesha, Wis.

Young people liked picnics. In the group *right*, the young man on the extreme right in the back row was John J. Pershing, popular instructor in military science at the University of Nebraska.

Courtesy, Nebraska State Historical Society, Lincoln

Spectator Sports

The observation train puffed along the course at New London as the Harvard and Yale crews of 1893 strained for victory. Yale won.

Harper's Weekly, July 1, 1893
Courtesy, Harper & Brothers, New York City

In the America's Cup races of 1893, *Vigilant* the American contender (shown *right*, leading), defeated the English yacht *Valkyrie II*.

At the New York Aquarium in old Castle Garden (*below*), those accomplished sportsmen, the seals, were always willing to perform. Few visitors to New York failed to call at the Aquarium.

Harper's Bazar, Oct. 21, 1893
Courtesy, Harper's Bazaar, New York City

Harper's Weekly, Sept. 30, 1893. Courtesy, Harper & Brothers, New York City

Industry

Despite the depression people had faith in industry and commerce. The news of developments in the Mesabi Range continued hopeful and exciting (see Vol. III, page 427).

To the *left* the steam shovel is loading ore at Biwabik Mine.

Courtesy, Minnesota Historical Society, St. Paul

At the *right* a similar big shovel bites into an ore dump at the Canton Mine.

Courtesy, Minnesota Historical Society, St. Paul

The Lake Superior Mine at Hibbing was another source of ore for the furnaces at Pittsburgh and Youngstown.

William F. Leggett and Frederick J. Chipman, *The City of Duluth and Environs.* 1895
Courtesy, The New-York Historical Society, New York City

Machinery

Believe in the machine, said the experts; given time, it would take care of everything. It would emancipate the workman and make everybody rich.

Courtesy, Chicago, Burlington & Quincy Railroad Company, Chicago, Ill.

Above was the latest type of steam locomotive, built for the Burlington at Paterson, N. J., in 1893.

Courtesy, Grace Line, New York City

The *Santa Rosa* of the Pacific Mail Steamship Line still carried rig for sails and was typical of modern steamships in 1893.

A gas tractor for general use was just appearing on the market.

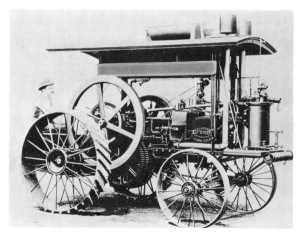

Courtesy, J. I. Case Company, Racine, Wis.

Lumber and Its Products

Looking around the country, the spectator of 1893 saw various sections progressing, and others at least holding their own in traditional trades and occupations.

Harper's Weekly, Mar. 25, 1893. Courtesy, Harper & Brothers, New York City

The loggers were cutting into the Minnesota pine forests.

Courtesy, North Carolina State Department of Archives and History, Raleigh

Rosin and turpentine continued to flow through the port of Wilmington, N. C.

Placid Indianapolis had a veneer factory near the Massachusetts Avenue depot.

VENEER WORKS, NEAR MASSACHUSETTS AVENUE DEPOT.

Indianapolis Illustrated. 1893
Courtesy, The Indiana Historical Society, Indianapolis

In the Old Dominion

Market carts continued to bring tobacco from the farms to the factories at Richmond, Va. (*above*). The reborn city had developed a large trade in flour as well as tobacco. The view *below* shows the industrial section of Richmond near the old Canal Basin, early in the Nineties.

Both illustrations on this page are by the courtesy of the Valentine Museum, Richmond, Va.

Power

In the Far West, history was being made at Redlands, Calif., where the first commercial polyphase power system began to operate in November, 1893. The generators were driven by one of the first Pelton impulse waterwheels.

Courtesy, General Electric Company, Schenectady, N. Y.

All was well with this Illinois blacksmith in 1893, but something was coming which would turn his prosperous trade into a thing of the past.

Courtesy, Mr. Myron F. Henkel, Springfield, Ill.

The flourishing Ohio refinery shown *left* stood to profit by the great impending change.

Courtesy, Standard Oil Company of Ohio, Cleveland

2

OLD ILLS AND NEW MEDICINES

Kelly's Army

The clouds of industrial disorder flashed a little lightning in the year 1894. "Armies" of the unemployed began to march on Washington.

From Oakland, Calif., General Kelly's group of 1,500 was given free transport as far as Council Bluffs, Iowa, where it arrived on April 15, as seen to the *right*.

Harper's Weekly, May 5, 1894
Courtesy, Harper & Brothers, New York City

Harper's Weekly, May 5, 1894
Courtesy, Harper & Brothers, New York City

Claiming that action for damages would lie against them if they conveyed destitute persons into Illinois, the Eastern railroads refused Kelly's demand for further transport. The "Army" set up Camp Despair (*left*) alongside the Rock Island tracks.

After a week of turmoil and dispute, Kelly's Army left Council Bluffs on foot. A mere remnant reached Washington and dispersed without a hearing.

Henry Vincent, *The Story of the Commonweal*. 1894
Courtesy, W. B. Conkey, Hammond, Ind.

Coxey's Army

Jacob S. Coxey, a prosperous businessman of Massillon, Ohio, led another of these "living petitions" in an effort to publicize his plan for giving work to the unemployed.

Henry Vincent, *The Story of the Commonweal.* 1894
Courtesy, W. B. Conkey, Hammond, Ind.

Calling itself "The Commonweal of Christ," Coxey's Army marched out of Massillon on Easter Sunday, 1894. Coxey, and his picturesque associate Carl Browne, hoped that 100,000 men would have joined the march by the time they reached Washington.

The school-children shown *right* came out to watch the ragged regiments pass through a Pennsylvania town.

Henry Vincent, *The Story of the Commonweal.* 1894
Courtesy, W. B. Conkey, Hammond, Ind.

Harper's Weekly, May 12, 1894
Courtesy, Harper & Brothers, New York City

Weary and hungry, the five hundred men who finished the march on May 1 stood quietly among thousands of curious spectators as Washington police led General Coxey away from the Capitol steps—his speech unread.

Cripple Creek

Not all the protests had overtones of mysticism: At Cripple Creek, Colo., the striking miners seized and fortified the mines.

Eleven hundred men were made Deputy Sheriffs on June 3, 1894, and mustered at the town of Divide for an attempt to recapture the mines. Company "M" of the Deputies is seen *left*.

Harper's Weekly, June 30, 1894.
Courtesy, Harper & Brothers, New York City

On the night of June 5, after a hazardous run in blacked-out freight cars and an eight-mile tramp over mountain roads, the Deputies laid siege to Bull Hill, where the strikers were in a strong position. A lively exchange of fire was interrupted by the arrival of the State Militia.

Harper's Weekly, June 30, 1894. Courtesy, Harper & Brothers, New York City

The Militia compelled the Deputies to withdraw and went into camp near the mines .

Mine owners at Leadville, Colo., attempted to bring in strike-breakers, and in retaliation the Coronado Mine (*right*) was blown up and burned.

Harper's Weekly, Dec. 12, 1896
Courtesy, Harper & Brothers, New York City

"Unlawful Obstructions"

In sympathy with striking Pullman employees, members of the American Railway Union refused to handle trains made up of Pullman cars.

Harper's Weekly, July 21, 1894
Courtesy, Harper & Brothers, New York City

On July 4, 1894, President Cleveland used the headline phrase quoted above in ordering Federal troops into the Chicago area. A blanket injunction had been issued against the strikers, and in the President's view the stoppage of the U. S. mail justified his action.

The strikers reacted as shown *left*, overturning cars and spiking switches.

The Seventh Cavalry (Custer's old command) patrolled the stockyards district as seen *right* in a sketch of Troop "K", drawn by Frederic Remington.

Harper's Weekly, July 21, 1894
Courtesy, Harper & Brothers, New York City

Harper's Weekly, July 28, 1894. Courtesy, Harper & Brothers, New York City

By July 20 the strike was broken and the troops withdrawn. But the ruins of burned rolling-stock cluttered the yards for miles.

In the City of Churches

Back East an equal bitterness was displayed in the street railway strike at Brooklyn, N. Y., early in 1895.

Harper's Weekly, Jan. 26, 1895
Courtesy, Harper & Brothers, New York City

The Remington sketch *above* shows the police clearing the way for a trolley-car. At the *left*, National Guardsmen are seen discouraging any demonstrations from houses. "Keep your windows down!"

In the picture *below*, a car is leaving the barn under military escort.

Harper's Weekly, Feb. 2, 1895
Courtesy, Harper & Brothers, New York City

Harper's Weekly, Feb. 2, 1895. *Courtesy*, Harper & Brothers, New York City

Silver Linings: The Motor Car

Despite unemployment and unrest, American inventiveness, by creating new needs and finding new uses for materials, was also creating new industries and new money.

The automobile was no one's "invention," but the United States took the lead in production of quantities of good gasoline cars at a low cost, so giving a higher acceleration to the great, national restlessness.

The circus poster to the *left* advertises the Duryea "horseless carriage" as an added attraction. This car won the Chicago *Times-Herald* contest in 1895, first road race ever run by automobiles in the United States.

Courtesy, General Motors Corporation, New York City

The first gasoline car to be driven in Detroit was the 1896 experimental model shown *right*, with one of the industry's pioneers, Charles B. King, at the controls.

Courtesy, Mr. Charles B. King, Larchmont, N. Y.

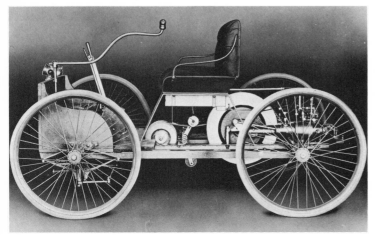

First of a long line was the 1896 Ford shown to the *left*.

Courtesy, Ford Motor Company, Dearborn, Mich.

Electric Power

For many years a symbol of honeymoon happiness, Niagara Falls was given a new role in 1895. Its waters were made to flow against the blades of turbines for the production of cheap electric power. In the picture to the *right*, three men are standing within the intake of a turbine under construction at the power station.

Harper's Weekly, Apr. 6, 1895
Courtesy, Harper & Brothers, New York City

The generators shown *below* began to feed 2,000 volts to transmission lines early in April. Each piece of equipment represented the solution of unprecedented technical problems.

Scribner's Magazine, March, 1896

The public continued to think of electric progress in terms of the "Wizard of Menlo Park," Thomas A. Edison, shown *above* early in 1896.

Courtesy, Westinghouse Electric Corporation, Pittsburgh, Pa.

Telephone

The while it perfected its local service, the telephone pressed on through the Nineties toward a declared goal: to send the human voice by wire across the continent.

The New York Police Department had linked its stations to Headquarters through a telephone switchboard as early as 1893.

The advantages of "Long Distance" telephoning were stressed in contemporary advertising.

Special pole-top distributors radiated lines to an increasing number of subscribers in city and country.

Flour Milling

In 1888 Duluth challenged the lead of Minneapolis in processing the hard wheat of Minnesota and the Dakotas. By 1894 the Imperial Mill at Duluth, shown *above*, was passing more than 8,000 barrels of flour a day through its grinding machinery (*below, left*) and sacking it on its packing floor (*below*), for deep-water shipment to the eastern markets and to Europe.

All illustrations on this page are from William F. Leggett and Frederick J. Chipman, *The City of Duluth and Environs.* 1895
Courtesy, The New-York Historical Society, New York City

Lake Ships

The flourishing industries of the Great Lakes region required transport for their goods, and Lake shipping became an industry in its own right.

The S. S. *North Land* (*left*) was built at Cleveland in 1895.

Courtesy, Mr. Thomas B. Dancey, Dearborn, Mich., and Capt. Fred A. Samuelson, Ludington, Mich.

To the *right* is an architect's drawing of the car ferry, *Ann Arbor.*

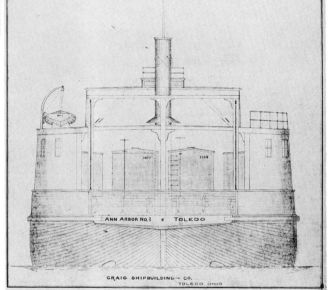

Courtesy, Mr. Joseph F. Rawlinson, Toledo, Ohio

The grain barge *Zenith City,* shown *left* as she loaded at the elevator, was in 1895 the largest freight steamer operating on fresh water in the United States. She was 400 feet over all, and carried 6,000 tons at an 18-foot draft.

William F. Leggett and Frederick J. Chipman, *The City of Duluth and Environs.* 1895
Courtesy, The New-York Historical Society, New York City

Fire Proofing

ἄσβεστος

Specimen of Asbestos in its natural state.

As there are many inferior imitations of our ASBESTOS manufactures, we call attention to the fact that all our goods bear our name or trade mark,

ASBESTOS

Nearly all our ASBESTOS MATERIALS are patented. We would, therefore, caution the public against the use of infringing articles.

H. W. JOHNS MANUFACTURING CO.

The uses of asbestos products were brought to public notice in dramatic fashion. A generation inured to theater disasters and panics were reassured by the legend on the curtain (*above*).

The page reproduced to the *left*, from a catalogue of 1894, commemorates one of the pioneers in asbestos manufacture.

Below is shown the original plant at Alexandria, Ind., where rock wool insulation was produced in an "artificial volcano."

Mail Order

Sears, Roebuck and Co. had expanded out of Minneapolis (see Volume III, page 421) and begun mass sales from Chicago.

They occupied the West Adams Street building shown *above* through 1895.

Above is shown a specimen page from an early issue of the "world's greatest silent salesman," famed in song and jest. To the *left* the cover of the 1896 issue is reproduced.

All illustrations on this page are by the *courtesy* of Sears, Roebuck and Co., Chicago, Ill.

Sidewalks of New York

The tide of immigration flowed through Ellis Island on to the streets of the metropolis.

The newsboy hawked his "poipers" in raucous tones that were reported everywhere as the true accent of New York.

The organ grinder and his wife with her little basket for coins were familiar street types. An agile monkey sometimes replaced Madame.

Shoe-shine boys of other races slouched in the steps of Horatio Alger's Yankee heroes at City Hall Park.

All illustrations on this page are by the *courtesy* of the Museum of the City of New York

Sidewalks of New York *(Continued)*

There was never a dull moment in New York's unceasing pageant.

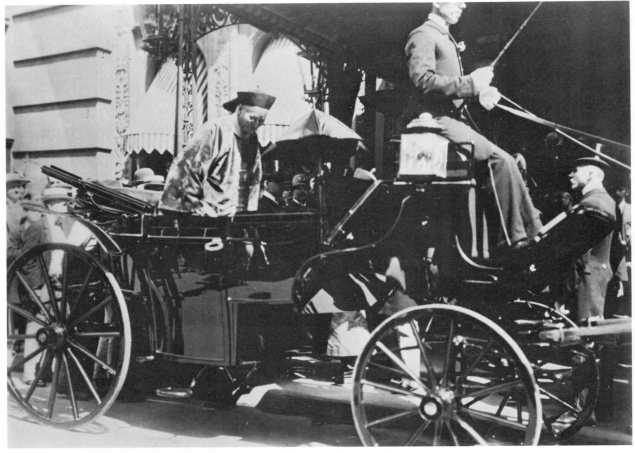

Courtesy, The Waldorf-Astoria, New York City

Above, His Excellency Li Hung Chang, Ambassador of China, Mandarin of the Yellow Button, arrived at the Waldorf in August, 1896. His visit was signalized by the refusal of six New York policemen to carry the "yellow haithen" about in a chair as his rank required.

But the workaday people of New York were not so much interested in exotic visitors as they were in the daily call of the postman and in the care the "white-wing" took of their own particular block.

Courtesy, Museum of the City of New York

Courtesy, Museum of the City of New York

Onward, Christian Soldiers

Harper's Weekly, Nov. 3, 1894.   *Courtesy,* Harper & Brothers, New York City

In the years after 1889, the work of the Salvation Army among the "down and outers" began to expand and command respect. In 1894, General William Booth, founder of the Army, addressed an audience at Carnegie Hall as shown *above*.

The 1894 headquarters of the Army in New York, shown *right*, housed administrative machinery for work in thirty-nine states and four hundred and thirty American cities.

Harper's Weekly, Mar. 30, 1895
Courtesy, Harper & Brothers, New York City

Statelier Mansions

New York and other cities were stretching up vertically as well as out laterally.

The Metropolitan Life Building bulked up beside Dr. Parkhurst's church on Madison Square and was vast and sumptuous in 1894. "The marble is marble all the way through," said the press, "and enough of it for the erection of half a dozen ordinary buildings." The Directors' Room, *below*, was wainscotted in solid mahogany.

Courtesy, The J. Clarence Davies Collection, Museum of the City of New York

Harper's Weekly, May 12, 1894
Courtesy, Harper & Brothers, New York City

Not two miles south of all this grandeur lay Chinatown and its surrounding slums.

Harper's Weekly, Feb. 29, 1896. Courtesy, Harper & Brothers, New York City

Main Street

To most Americans in 1894 Main Street was still the center of life, economic and social.

To the *right* is Main Street in Francestown, N. H.

W. R. Cochrane and G. K. Wood, *History of Francestown, New Hampshire.* 1895
Courtesy, The New-York Historical Society, New York City

Courtesy, Iowa State Department of History and Archives, Des Moines

The pictures to the *left* and *below* were taken on Main Street in Brooklyn, Iowa. Note the horse rigs of various types, the board sidewalk, the shop fronts.

Courtesy, Iowa State Department of History and Archives, Des Moines

The Good Old Summertime

In each section of the country, June signalled an exodus from city and suburb to resorts of more or less pretension. Contingent on pocketbook and degree of social ambition, the wilted businessman on his holiday followed mother and the girls to the particular spot they favored.

He might relax to music amid the faded splendor of Saratoga (*right*).

Or he might be limited to spending an evening at a Coney Island music hall (*below*).

Harper's Weekly. Aug. 1, 1896
Courtesy, Harper & Brothers, New York City

Scribner's Magazine, July, 1896

The same urge on a higher level of display peopled the marble palaces of Newport. A sense of attainment gave an added zest to the music at the Casino (*right*).

Harper's Bazar, Nov. 9, 1895
Courtesy, Harper's Bazaar, New York City

Peacock Alley

In the cities, hotels catered to a growing number of people who found it convenient to entertain in public, and whose egos welcomed a certain notoriety.

The corridor of New York's Waldorf-Astoria (*right*) became legendary as a place for genteel display.

The Roof Garden

attracted a somewhat different clientele (*below*).

Harper's Bazar, Mar. 21, 1896
Courtesy, Harper's Bazaar, New York City

Harper's Weekly, Sept. 26, 1896. *Courtesy*, Harper & Brothers, New York City

Genteel Eating

Harper's Weekly, Nov. 21, 1896. *Courtesy*, Harper & Brothers, New York City

After the Horse Show, supper parties thronged the ballroom of the Waldorf-Astoria as seen *above* in Smedley's drawing.

Sumptuous Sitting

Note the antimacassars on the back of chairs in the parlor of the Southern Hotel, St. Louis, shown *right*.

Courtesy, Missouri Historical Society, St. Louis

An interesting reflection of popular taste for things Oriental is seen in the public room *left*—a "Turkish Den."

Courtesy, Missouri Historical Society, St. Louis

Bon Ton

The sports of society (in the narrow sense) took on an antiquarian air. There was an irony in the preoccupation of leisured folk with coaching and blooded horses on the eve of the motor age.

To the *right*, a lady is handling the ribbons at Newport; *below* is a sketch at the 1895 Horse Show in old Madison Square Garden.

Harper's Weekly, Nov. 16, 1895
Courtesy, Harper & Brothers, New York City

Harper's Weekly, Aug. 21, 1895
Courtesy, Harper & Brothers, New York City

A little after noon on Nov. 6, 1895, Consuelo, eldest daughter of W. K. Vanderbilt, was united in the holy bonds of matrimony at St. Thomas's, New York, to His Grace, the Duke of Marlborough. The bridal procession is shown *right*, as it left the chancel.

The tendency of American wealth to seek European titles for its daughters was a phenomenon of the day that provided rich material for social historians and novelists.

Harper's Weekly, Nov. 16, 1895
Courtesy, Harper & Brothers, New York City

Costume for Occasions

The lady of 1895 and 1896 was most discreet in her choice of clothes for definite occasions. The line between good and bad taste was only vaguely appreciated by the masculine mind, but knowledge of its precise point of drawing was the most important part of a lady's education.

Harper's Bazar, Dec. 8, 1894
Courtesy, Harper's Bazaar, New York City

The ball dress *above* was a creation by Doucet.

Harper's Bazar, Aug. 11, 1894
Courtesy, Harper's Bazaar, New York City

Ivory white and écru were combined in the lawn-party gown shown *above*.

When dresses like these had done their deadly work, the occasion to the *left* was distinguished by appropriate costume. Reading from left to right: an attendant; the mother of the bride; the bride herself; a bridesmaid.

Harper's Bazar, Aug. 29, 1896
Courtesy, Harper's Bazaar, New York City

Harper's Bazar, Sept. 8, 1894
Courtesy, Harper's Bazaar, New York City

Mourning bonnets were *chic* but unmistakeable.

Accessories

A proper turn-out required equal taste in choice of accessories.

Harper's Bazar, Apr. 21, 1894
Courtesy, Harper's Bazaar, New York City

Harper's Bazar, Sept. 19, 1896
Courtesy, Harper's Bazaar, New York City

Harper's Bazar, Dec. 28, 1895
Courtesy, Harper's Bazaar, New York City

Harper's Bazar, Apr. 14,
1894
Courtesy, Harper's
Bazaar, New York City

The parasol shown was "of green and pink shot moiré with a deep flounce of pink chiffon; the handle, a Dresden China Knob."

Reading down from left to right, the boots shown were a "carriage boot with kid top and patent leather tip and vamp"; a "dress slipper of black satin with papillon rosette"; and a "bicycle boot of American kid."

The corset shown was "designed to direct rather than trammel the figure," and made much of the fact that it had been fitted on a living model.

Harper's Bazar, Nov. 17, 1894
Courtesy, Harper's Bazaar, New York City

1895 styles in evening coiffure favored the Louis XVI fashion. The costume muff of black velvet had its ruffles faced with white moiré and "amid a drapery of white lace posed a black bird with white wings."

The Mere Man

With the exception of the professed "dude," the man was content to provide a sober background for feminine elegance.

Courtesy, Nevada State Historical Society, Reno

Above, a Western family poses gloomily in their 1895 best.

The city gentleman shown *left* wore his Sunday clothes on a country stroll because it was Sunday.

Courtesy, Associate Editor

The "New Woman"

The progress of the American woman toward emancipation, the franchise and equal opportunity in the professions was evident in this catch-phrase of the day and in the type of woman it was invented to describe.

"How they would have gazed!" editorialized the artist in his 1896 sketch to the *right*.

Harper's Bazar, Mar. 14, 1896
Courtesy, Harper's Bazaar, New York City

Harper's Bazar, June 20, 1896
Courtesy, Harper's Bazaar, New York City

There was no longer any element of novelty about the college commencements of young ladies. To the *left* is shown the Barnard Class of '96.

To the *right*, a lady reporter is seen interviewing Chauncey M. Depew in his New York Central Railroad office.

Alexander Black, *Miss Jerry*. 1895

Muscling In

Courtesy, Public Relations Office, University of Nebraska, Lincoln

Other colleges were beginning to follow the lead given by the University of Nebraska in competitive athletics for women.

Courtesy, Public Relations Office, University of Nebraska, Lincoln

The New York stage, prompt to capitalize on new trends in society, offered the play advertised *left*. Note the *Yellow Book* influence on the drawing in the poster.

Scribner's Magazine, October, 1895

The "Working Girl"

The demand for "equal rights" was not voiced entirely by the girl undergraduates or the frequenters of culture clubs.

The girls who worked in mills and shops began to raise their voices.

Courtesy, Westinghouse Electric Corporation, Pittsburgh, Pa.

In the picture *left* a group of laundresses are shown "sitting-down" in support of the 1896 garment workers' strike.

Scribner's Magazine, October, 1896

Ladies took a prominent part in this strike meeting at Cooper Union, New York City.

Scribner's Magazine, October, 1896

Characters

Courtesy, Scribner Art File

The gas-man to the *left* was typical of the plain, hard-working citizen who plodded in a rut set for him by circumstances. But, as seen *below,* there were also workmen who turned away from the bench to think—ingenious men who built up the national reputation for mechanical skill and the "know-how" of production.

Sport

The first Women's Golf Championship Tour-
nament was played off at Meadow Brook, Long
Island, in 1895, and was won by Mrs. Charles
S. Brown (*right*) of the Shinnecock Hills Club.

Harper's Bazar, Nov. 30, 1895
Courtesy, Harper's Bazaar, New York City

Harper's Weekly, Aug. 31, 1895
Courtesy, Harper & Brothers, New York City

Tennis continued to be a favorite sport,
but its growing popularity with the
week-ending vulgar caused a little head
shaking.

There seemed little possibility of a popular vogue for polo, however. *Below* is seen an "out
of bounds" at the Rockaway Hunt Club.

Harper's Weekly, Aug. 10, 1895. *Courtesy,* Harper & Brothers, New York City

Sport (Continued)

Stories of the superior stamina, skill and achievement of old-time athletes can be had from our anecdotal elders at the drop of a hat.

Courtesy, Purdue University, Latayette, Ind.

All football teams of the Nineties were mighty, and young men on strange contraptions (*below*) set records for all time.

Harper's Bazar, Mar. 14, 1896
Courtesy, Harper's Bazaar, New York City

The athlete in training frequently suffers from exhaustion, and then from an inordinate desire or thirst for intoxicating beverages. Such beverages at such a time retard his training and do him infinite harm. All trainers of experience recognize this, and those who have tried this new wine on their men say that it answers the purpose admirably, preventing the exhaustion and also the dangerous thirst alluded to. Mr. M. C. Murphy, trainer for Yale University and for the New York Athletic Club has said:

"I used Vino Kolafra freely myself before giving it to my men. It acts at once on the nervous system, and in this way braces up the muscles. More, it keeps them braced, and, besides giving the system an immediate lift, improves the general health. I know of nothing except Vino Kolafra, besides food, sleep, exercise, and good habits, which can be conscientiously given by a trainer to his men. It certainly is a remarkable drug, or food, I leave others to decide which. I can only speak as to its effects."

Mr. Murphy then went on to enumerate the benefits which resulted from the use of Vino Kolafra. He said that when a man used it he could not train him tired, as the wine appeared to kill fatigue. He found it also an aid to digestion and an alleviation of thirst. "It gives," he said, "staying power. A man can run harder and longer; a crew can row faster and longer. The simple fact is, it adds as much power to the muscles as coal does to an engine. Again, in keeping the pulse even, the heart regular, the temperature normal, the nervous system properly keyed up, it is a wonderful help in discipline. Overdrinking and over-eating are the two principal factors adverse to health with which the trainer has to deal."

The explanation of these feats and others (see page 25) is given on high authority in the advertisement *left.*

Courtesy, Johnson & Johnson,
New Brunswick, N. J.

Harper's Bazar, Mar. 14, 1896
Courtesy, Harper's Bazaar, New York City

Bicycling

This sport, introduced as far back as the late 1860's, reached a peak of popularity between 1894 and the turn of the century.

Proper costume was an important factor for lady cyclists as observed in the 1894 sketch shown *right*.

Harper's Bazar, July 14, 1894
Courtesy, Harper's Bazaar, New York City

The Buffalo, N. Y., father pictured to the *left* devised this rig to solve the perennial problem of keeping an eye on the children. He made regular runs to Niagara Falls.

Harper's Weekly, May 23, 1896
Courtesy, Harper & Brothers, New York City

Cyclists are seen *right* arriving at the Newport Casino.

Harper's Bazar, Oct. 5, 1895
Courtesy, Harper's Bazaar, New York City

Outdoor Togs

Feminine participation in outdoor life was reflected in the *mode* of the years 1894 to 1896. The fashion sketches shown *below* were suggested as appropriate for:

Swimming

Yachting

Harper's Bazar, May 30, 1896
Courtesy, Harper's Bazaar, New York City

Cycling

Harper's Bazar, June 30, 1894
Courtesy, Harper's Bazaar, New York City

Mountain Climbing

Harper's Bazar, Apr. 14, 1894
Courtesy, Harper's Bazaar, New York City

Harper's Bazar, June 1, 1895
Courtesy, Harper's Bazaar, New York City

The Athletic Club

The businessman and professional man of the period who did not care to let his waistline lapse too early into middle-aged dignity joined an athletic club and worked at sport in his leisure hours.

Baseball was popular at the Crescent Club (*right*).

Scribner's Magazine, July, 1895

Harper's Weekly, Jan. 19, 1895
Courtesy, Harper & Brothers, New York City

Cycle Clubs were born out of the prevalent bicycle fad.

Cricket was played in the United States. The sketch *right* was made in 1895 at the Richmond County Cricket Club, New York.

Scribner's Magazine, July, 1895

Amateur Entertainment

The humble minstrel show and dance was popular everywhere, but the Richmond, Va., ladies shown *below* aimed higher. For the Kirmess of 1896 they performed a classic Grecian dance.

Courtesy, San Mateo County Historical Association, San Mateo, Calif.

Courtesy, The Valentine Museum, Richmond, Va.

In the picture *below*, a Springfield, Ill., family prepares to enjoy a "musical evening" at home.

Courtesy, Mr. Myron F. Henkel, Springfield, Ill.

Everyday Pleasures

The soda at the drug-store fountain, the drive in the surrey, the trolley-party delighted many more people than the sophisticated amusements already shown on pages 49 to 51.

Courtesy, Ravenswood-Lake View Historical Association, sponsored by The Chicago Public Library, Ill.

Courtesy, Ravenswood-Lake View Historical Association, sponsored by The Chicago Public Library, Ill.

Courtesy, Mr. Myron F. Henkel, Springfield, Ill.

Days Out

Parties of friends drove or walked out into the deep, sweet-smelling country to spread the contents of picnic-baskets where ants and other small intruders could share the good things.

Courtesy, Nebraska State Historical Society, Lincoln

Boys and girls together on the broad plains of Nebraska!

But the picnic shown *right* on Lake Superior's north shore was strictly feminine and juvenile.

Courtesy, St. Louis County Historical Society, Duluth, Minn.

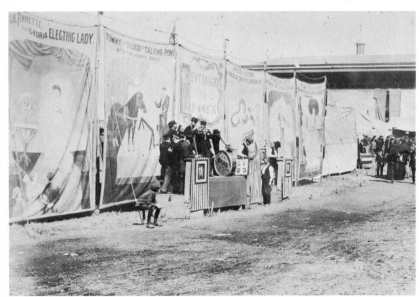

The Midway at the Illinois State Fair of 1896 featured "Annette the Electric Lady" and "Tommy the Talking Pony." The advertisements of Captain Ament's show claimed that the exhibits were "strictly moral and elevating."

Courtesy, Mr. Myron F. Henkel, Springfield, Ill.

See America First

Hayden Valley.

One of the

Very Beautiful Sights

In the

YELLOWSTONE PARK

tour is that of this very lovely valley. It lies between the Yellowstone Lake and Grand Canyon. It is softly undulating, long and wide, covered with luxuriant grass, watered by crystal streams. The mountains form a wall about it. The river winds across it like an emerald serpent. The scene is of a highly poetic cast.

William F. Leggett and Frederick J. Chipman, *The City of Duluth and Environs*. 1895
Courtesy, The New-York Historical Society, New York City

Railroads advertised the wonders of the West, and each season found a new crop of trippers in the Yellowstone National Park.

Courtesy, National Park Service, Chicago, Ill.

Stages brought them from the railroad station up to the Mammoth Hot Springs Hotel.

Courtesy, National Park Service, Chicago, Ill.

They camped out in appropriate costume where, only twenty years before, the Indians had set their lodges.

Courtesy, National Park Service, Chicago, Ill.

An excursion steamer ferried them across Yellowstone Lake to West Thumb.

The Three "R's"

The germs of progressive education were being incubated at the University of Chicago laboratory school at the very time the pictures below were taken.

An Illinois class stands and sits in regimented ranks.

Courtesy, Ravenswood-Lake View Historical Association, sponsored by The Chicago Public Library, Ill.

In California, this graduating group had survived its regimented schooling with obvious success.

Courtesy, Pomona Public Library, Calif.

And here is a typical Mid-West faculty group — no doubt regimented also.

Courtesy, Ravenswood-Lake View Histrical Association, sponsored by The Chicago Public Library, Ill.

The University

In May, 1896, the corner-stone of Schermerhorn Hall at Columbia University was laid. Just behind, and to the right of the gentleman with the white chin whiskers, marches the then Dean of the faculty of Philosophy, Dr. Nicholas Murray Butler.

Courtesy, Columbiana, Columbia University, New York City

As universities expanded physically, a taste for luxury began to develop in American under-graduates, and alumni were heard lamenting the good old Spartan days.

Even in the rugged Mid-West, where undergraduates had once rejoiced in breaking the ice in the wash-bucket on winter mornings, the 1894 advertisement *below, left* warned "You can't draw the line too sharply in ordering Commencement attire."

Courtesy, Purdue University, Lafayette, Ind.

Scribner's Magazine, July, 1897

The contemporary sketch *above* purports to show a typical room at Yale in 1896.

Baker's Bread

Another trend in American life is well illustrated in the baker's advertisement *below*, where grandma, her head drooping sadly, perjures herself to save the coming generation from kitchen drudgery.

"YES ITS BETTER BREAD THAN I CAN MAKE"

LANGDON BAKERY, U. S. BAKING CO.,
CINCINNATI, O.

Harper's Weekly, May 12, 1894
Courtesy, Harper & Brothers, New York City

The girls at Purdue, shown *below*, were members of the college Cooking Club, and were by no means willing to regard the kitchen as an outmoded relic of barbarism.

Courtesy, Purdue University, Lafayette, Ind.

Railroad Developments

Engineers were wondering in 1895 just how long it would take before electric locomotives would supersede steam on the nation's roads.

To the *right* is seen the Baltimore and Ohio's electric locomotive No. 1 hauling a train into Mount Royal station in 1895.

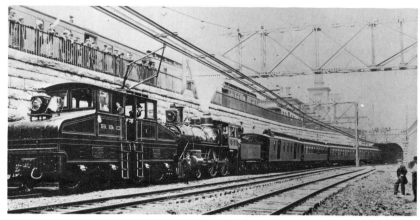

Courtesy, Scribner Art File

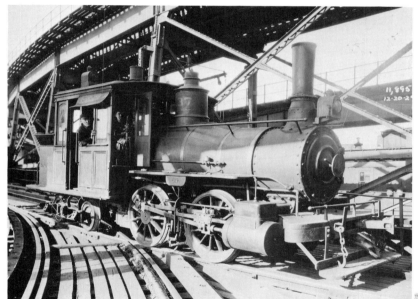

Courtesy, Board of Transportation of The City of New York

Already the jaunty little steam engines used on the New York elevated railways had been replaced by electric cars. To the *left*, one of the last "donkeys" heads toward the junk-pile.

Manufacturers were experimenting with use of internal combustion engines on the rails. The model shown *right* was built in 1896.

Courtesy, Fairbanks, Morse & Co., Chicago, Ill.

Road Work

Even where the new automobile seldom went, passable roads were necessary—for getting the corn and hogs to town. *Below* is a township grader at work on a dirt road.

Courtesy, Public Roads Administration, Washington, D. C.

Paving

Courtesy, Mrs. Ruth Locker MacDonald, Two Harbors, Minn.

Many small towns were adding paved streets to cement sidewalks.

The "New Navy"

The Navy began to revive in morale after a long period of decay and neglect.

Great credit for the revival must go to the Naval War College at Newport (*right*), where Alfred T. Mahan delivered his famous lectures on the influence of sea power, and senior officers were trained in working as a team.

Harper's Weekly, Apr. 11, 1896
Courtesy, Harper & Brothers, New York City

Harper's Weekly, Sept. 7, 1895. Courtesy, Harper & Brothers, New York City

Above is Zogbaum's sketch of the North Atlantic squadron at Bar Harbor in 1895.

Internal Improvements

Harper's Weekly, Sept. 1, 1894
Courtesy, Harper & Brothers, New York City

The Chicago Drainage Canal, later to be the subject of much litigation, was under construction (*left*).

The *Goldenrod* and her crew plied the Ohio River and took care of the light-houses along its course.

Harper's Bazar, Nov. 21, 1896
Courtesy, Harper's Bazaar, New York City

The Library of Congress was nearing completion. In the picture *left*, men are seen at work in the special marble-cutting shop where the carvings were executed.

Harper's Weekly, Dec. 28, 1895
Courtesy, Harper & Brothers, New York City

Irrigation

Although real progress on a national scale awaited the Reclamation Act of 1902, the Carey Act had encouraged some States to reclaim arid lands, and there was considerable private activity. There was also considerable scoffing at the idea.

Harper's Weekly, Oct. 5, 1895. Courtesy, Harper & Brothers, New York City

Above, a young orchard is rising in California on irrigated soil.

The picture *right*, near Larned, Kans., shows windmill pumps filling an irrigation reservoir.

Harper's Weekly, Apr. 2, 1898
Courtesy, Harper & Brothers, New York City

The wasteway shown *left* was part of the Colorado system for diverting water from the Big Laramie into the Cache La Poudre River.

Harper's Weekly, June 12, 1897
Courtesy, Harper & Brothers, New York City

Fruit Growing

Irrigation was not the only factor in the rise of large-scale fruit growing for the market. Commercial canning and refrigerator freight cars played a great part.

Harper's Weekly, Aug. 24, 1895. Courtesy, Harper & Brothers, New York City

Above is shown a California vineyard in 1895 under irrigation.

To the *left*, strawberries are being picked near Lawtey, Fla. *Below* is a sketch of cold-storage fruit arriving at the New York terminal.

Harper's Weekly, May 9, 1896. Courtesy, Harper & Brothers, New York City

Public Services

There was constant improvement in local services affecting property, health and the culture of the mind.

Small-town fire brigades took pride in their smartness and their care of equipment.

Courtesy, San Mateo County Historical Association, San Mateo, Calif.

In company with many other cities, Duluth, Minn., took pride in its Public Library, the well-trained staff, and the expanding service to neighboring communities without library facilities.

William F. Leggett and Frederick J. Chipman, *The City of Duluth and Environs.* 1895
Courtesy, The New-York Historical Society, New York City

Post Graduate Hospital, New York City, was still pioneering in free medical and surgical treatment to babies in special wards. An incubator is shown *right.*

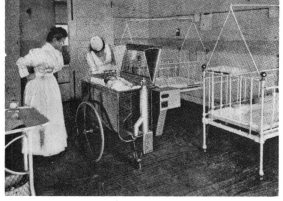

Harper's Bazar, Sept. 1, 1894
Courtesy, Harper's Bazaar, New York City

On the Eve

Though a bitterly contested election was in prospect for 1896, plain people went quietly about their business. Nature plodded her accustomed round as if nothing were amiss.

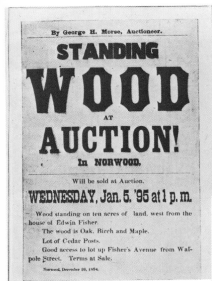

Highway on Auction Day

Wood Auctions were held in New England.

Harper's Weekly, Jan. 11, 1896
Courtesy, Harper & Brothers, New York City

The river boats dropped downstream to tie up at the foot of Canal Street, New Orleans.

Courtesy, Board of Commissioners of the Port of
New Orleans, La.

Hammock and garden chairs were set out on the neat lawns of serene Mid-Western homes.

Courtesy, Mr. Myron F. Henkel, Springfield, Ill.

National Issues

Gold was the sole medium of exchange whereby a sound economy could be maintained. Silver was the edged tool with which Socialists would bring the nation to ruin. On the other hand, gold was the sinister fetish which gave power to Wall Street and the Trusts: Silver was the poor man's friend. On these simplifications of the true issues, the Republican and Democratic parties took their stand, nominated candidates and fought the campaign.

The depression years had been years of Democratic administration. When the Republican Party held its convention that June in the St. Louis auditorium shown *right*, Mark Hanna boasted that any Republican could be elected.

Courtesy, Missouri Historical Society, St. Louis

Since 1890 Hanna had been grooming his friend, William McKinley, for the nomination; by shrewd management before the convention met, he won nomination for his friend on the first ballot. McKinley proposed to make a "front porch" campaign.

Courtesy, Scribner Art File

Cross of Gold

Three weeks later, when the Democrats held their convention at Chicago, it was clear that silver sentiment would sweep the convention. Delegates committed to free coinage of silver controlled the committees, but there was no outstanding and inevitable candidate.

Richard Bland had been active in organizing the silver forces, and his identification with the cause made his nomination a possibility. But a silver delegate from Nebraska, William Jennings Bryan (seen *right* in his favorite picture), rose to make the closing plea for silver before 20,000 yelling spectators.

When he ceased, the nomination was his after five ballots.

Courtesy, Mrs. Ruth Bryan Rohde, Ossining, N. Y.

W. B. Byars, *An American Commoner.* 1900. Courtesy, E. W. Stephens Company, Columbia, Mo.

William J. Bryan, *The First Battle.* 1896. Courtesy, W. B. Conkey Company, Hammond, Ind.

Above is shown the Democratic Convention of 1896 which thrilled as one man to Bryan's closing words ". . . you shall not crucify mankind upon a cross of gold."

Campaign of 1896

In support of McKinley and the Gold Standard, men argued and fought; they organized "Sound Money" clubs and paraded through the nation's streets.

At the *right*, New York lawyers have left their panelled offices to witness their faith in gold.

Courtesy, The New-York Historical Society, New York City

Courtesy, The Indiana Historical Society, Indianapolis

Residents of Delphi, Ind. (*above*), marched under the banner "Vote Bryan and a Panic."

Golden Voice

Bryan waged a whirlwind campaign that made Republicans doubt the wisdom of the "front porch" strategy.

William J. Bryan, *The First Battle.* 1896
Courtesy, W. B. Conkey Company, Hammond, Ind.

He traveled day and night, speaking twenty times a day to great crowds and small.

People of Wellsville, Ohio (*right*), listened to the golden voice.

William J. Bryan, *The First Battle.* 1896
Courtesy, W. B. Conkey Company, Hammond, Ind.

On Oct. 23, 1896, the Springfield, Ill., wheelmen, to celebrate his arrival in their town, performed at the head of a great parade.

Courtesy, Mr. Myron F. Henkel, Springfield, Ill.

3

THE IMPERIAL EXPERIMENT

After a campaign almost evangelical in fervor, the nation went to the polls in November, 1896, and elected William McKinley President with 271 electoral votes to Bryan's 176.

Harper's Weekly, Mar. 13, 1897.
Courtesy, Harper & Brothers, New York City

The new President was sworn into office on Mar. 4, 1897. A photograph of the traditional ceremony is shown *above*. He was committed by his statements and his party's platform to high, protective tariffs; to the maintenance of the gold standard; and the denial of the government's right to control or discipline business.

Courtesy, Scribner Art File

A short man, the President (*above*) held himself rigidly erect.

The Gay World

Freed of the nagging threat to comfortable living represented by the embattled Democrats and their "peerless leader," certain elements of society blossomed at such functions as the Bradley Martin ball shown *below*, denounced as shameful waste by the reformers of the time.

Harper's Weekly, Feb. 20, 1897. *Courtesy*, Harper & Brothers, New York City

Harper's Bazar, Feb. 5, 1898
Courtesy, Harper's Bazaar, New York City

Atlantic City, New Jersey's year-round resort (*above*), was a favorite place for relaxing.

The Easter Parade on New York's Fifth Avenue (*right*) was as ever a brilliant display.

Harper's Bazar, Apr. 9, 1898
Courtesy, Harper's Bazaar, New York City

Fun on a Budget

The Dingley Tariff might save the country, or ruin it; but ordinary folk were not too deeply stirred by the prospect.

The circus came to Boonville, Mo., as usual (*right*).

On Sunday you could hire a boat for a row on the lake in Forest Park, St. Louis (*below*).

Courtesy, Charles van Ravenswaay Collection, Missouri Historical Society, St. Louis

Courtesy, Missouri Historical Society, St. Louis

Harper's Weekly, July 24, 1897. *Courtesy,* Harper & Brothers, New York City

And in late afternoon the band played beside Prospect Park lake at Brooklyn, N. Y.

Popular Art

Courtesy, Mr. Myron F. Henkel, Springfield, Ill.

Public music was not necessarily furnished by a professional band. The Watch Factory Band shown *left* was the pride of Springfield, Ill., and made concert tours through the Mid-West and South.

The ladies of Salem, Mass., enjoyed dressing up in their grandmothers' clothes and presenting "living tableaux" for a church benefit as the picture *below* indicates.

From a photograph by Frank Cousins. *Courtesy*, The Essex Institute, Salem, Mass.

Future Presidents

Sandlot, District School and City Park served as training grounds for future citizens.

One of the future Ivy League half-backs shown *right* was recovering from the mumps.

Courtesy, Mr. Myron F. Henkel, Springfield, Ill.

For all their troubles with mortgages and drought, farmers of western Kansas kept up their schools and their hopes for their children.

Courtesy, Dr. Robert Taft, University of Kansas, Lawrence

City children took the air under nursie's eye, as in the view *right* of Monroe Park, Richmond, Va.

Courtesy, The Valentine Museum, Richmond, Va.

What Made It Go

The willingness and ability of people in small communities to use their purchasing power for self-improvement made possible the spectacular activities of big business.

Courtesy, Public Roads Administration, Washington, D. C.

In the picture *left*, Indiana farmers in 1898 are celebrating the opening of the first Rural Free Delivery route in their neighborhood. People like these gave economic life to the towns where they traded.

Their problems made work for the local courts and occupied the lawyers who practiced in town. In the picture *right*, an Illinois judge counsels a litigant.

Courtesy, Mr. Myron F. Henkel, Springfield, Ill.

The prosperity of his rural neighbors and clients determined the success or failure of the town banker shown *left* with his staff.

Courtesy, Mr. Myron F. Henkel, Springfield, Ill.

Homes

Courtesy, Mrs. Frank Ewing, Grand Rapids, Mich.

Many farm homes of 1897 were substantial, well-tended and comfortable, as seen *above* in a picture taken near Woodbridge, Mich.

The street in Cheyenne, Wyo., pictured *below* was typical of thousands of "home town" streets of the time.

Courtesy, Mr. J. E. Stimson and the Wyoming State Library and State Historical Department, Cheyenne

Homes—Interior

Comfort was the primary consideration in middle-class home furnishings.

The living-room corner in Logansport, Ind. (*left*), displays many typical articles of 1897 furnishing. Note the antimacassar on the back of father's rocking chair; the starched lace curtains; the spool-legged table; the "tidies" and the bric-a-brac.

The bedroom from the same house had a fancy carpet, a Grand Rapids "set" of bed and bureau, and a base-burner stove for warmth.

Both illustrations on this page are by the *courtesy* of Miss Etta Wright and The Indiana Historical Society Library, Indianapolis

College Girls

The New Woman at college took part in traditional observances more ladylike than the cane-rushes and water-fights of the men's colleges.

At Vassar, the Daisy Chain was borne solemnly by the Sophomore Class (*right*). At Wellesley, the Seniors rolled hoops (*below*).

Harper's Bazar, June 11, 1898
Courtesy, Harper's Bazaar, New York City

Harper's Bazar, June 11, 1898. *Courtesy, Harper's Bazaar, New York City*

Sororities flourished. The girls shown *right* were Kappa Kappa Gammas at Nebraska.

*Courtesy, Nebraska State
Historical Society, Lincoln*

Aspiration to the Arts

Musical and sketching societies interested the boys and girls of the Nineties.

Courtesy, Mr. Myron F. Henkel, Springfield, Ill.

Mandolin clubs were popular at schools and colleges.

To the *right* is shown a college Art Club off for a day's work with pencil and watercolor.

Courtesy, Agnes Scott College, Decatur, Ga.

Courtesy, Mr. Myron F. Henkel, Springfield, Ill.

Yet such a seemingly unaesthetic group as the 1897 High School Track Team shown *left* produced a celebrated American poet. Vachel Lindsay stands second from the right.

The Gibson Influence

The people in pictures drawn by Charles Dana Gibson became models for the appearance and manners of a whole generation. His clean-cut square-jawed young men of action put the moustached exquisite wholly in the shade, and his queenly women were ideals equally for the college girl and the milliner's apprentice.

Scribner's Magazine, February, 1897

Scribner's Magazine, June, 1897

The three illustrations on this page are typical of Gibson's work as a magazine illustrator.

Scribner's Magazine, May, 1897

Fore!

The game of golf was no longer an amiable eccentricity and had become sufficiently popular to attract the attention of one of the foremost illustrators of the day. The three sketches *below*, from three different periodicals, are the work of A. B. Frost.

"Dormy Two" (*left*).

Scribner's Magazine, October, 1897

Left, "A Drive." The picture *below* is captioned "Golf Terms Illustrated: A Hole in One," and is presumably the first use of this wheeze by any humorist.

GOLF TERMS ILLUSTRATED—"A HOLE IN ONE."

Harper's Bazar, Nov. 3, 1894
Courtesy, Harper's Bazaar, New York City

Harper's Weekly, May 21, 1898
Courtesy, Harper & Brothers, New York City

Food Retailing

The local storekeeper was not as yet aware of the formidable competition he was to receive from chain stores, and he was inclined to be somewhat contemptuous of their cash policy and their advertising methods.

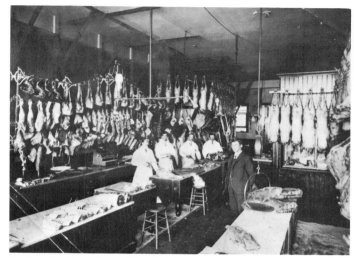

A large retail meat-market is shown *right*; the meat was shipped to it in refrigerator cars.

Courtesy, San Mateo County Historical Association, San Mateo, Calif.

In the picture *left*, an early store of a famous chain is seen as it was in 1898. Note the sandwich man in the center and the display of lamps, fans and other "premiums" to be given the customers.

Courtesy, The Great Atlantic and Pacific Tea Company, New York City

Packaged and canned foods were fighting uphill against popular prejudice. In the picture *right*, strawberries are being examined at the receiving platform of a packer of jams and relishes.

Courtesy, H. J. Heinz Company, Pittsburgh, Pa.

Advertising

The germs of later "mass appeals" were lurking in advertisements of the late Nineties.

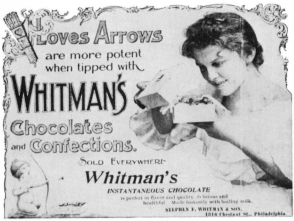

Courtesy, N. W. Ayer & Son, Inc., Philadelphia, Pa.

Candy manufacturers had discovered the pretty-girl angle (*above*).

But Buffalo Bill's show stuck to the tried and true, with a concession to the war spirit of 1898.

Harper's Weekly, Dec. 17, 1898
Courtesy, Harper & Brothers, New York City

The indorsers who approved of the patent-medicine in the ad *above* were high and mighty enough for anyone.

Courtesy of the Bella C. Landauer Collection in The New-York Historical Society, New York City

Motor manufacturers were stressing luxury, appearance and ease of operation (*right*).

Harper's Weekly, May 21, 1898
Courtesy, Harper & Brothers, New York City

Electric Power—Applied

From power stations at newly-harnessed Niagara and elsewhere, electricity at reduced cost was available for commercial applications on a vast scale.

The feeders shown *right* were built in 1897 to carry ten thousand volts from Niagara to the step-down transformers of the Buffalo street-railway system.

Harper's Weekly, June 5, 1897
Courtesy, Harper & Brothers, New York City

Courtesy, General Electric Company, Schenectady, N. Y.

Streets in cities, large and small, were lighted by arc-lamps like those shown on the assembly racks *left*.

The applications of electric power were not always on the grand scale. One of the first electrically operated coffee-mills is shown *right*—also a development of 1897.

W. H. Ukers, *All About Coffee.* 1935
Courtesy, The Tea and Coffee Trade Journal,
New York City

"Number, Please—"

Patent strife and public incredulity were by 1897 only bad memories. The telephone industry pressed on to wider expansion of services and a more efficient organization.

The Harlem "Central" in New York City is seen *left* as it was in 1897. The woman seated beyond the manager was "Information"; the board at the far end of the room was the toll-board for out-of-town calls.

Courtesy, American Telephone and Telegraph Company, New York City

At the *right* is shown the auditors' office of the New York Telephone Company, around 1897

Courtesy, American Telephone and Telegraph Company, New York City

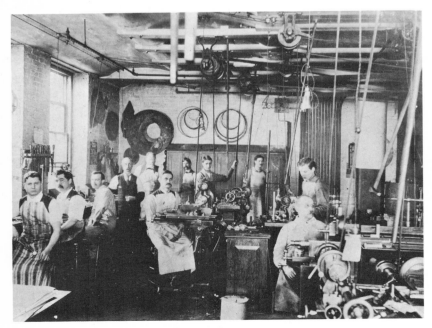

Technical improvements kept tool-workers like the Chicago crew *left* hard at work turning blue-prints into practical form.

Courtesy, Western Electric Company, New York City

Electric Taxicabs

In early spring, 1897, the Electric Vehicle Company started cab service in New York City.

The style of the cabs followed conventional patterns. To the *right* is a battery-powered coach, and *below* is a close cousin of the venerable hansom, photographed later in the season.

Courtesy, Museum of the City of New York

Courtesy, The J. Clarence Davies Collection, Museum of the City of New York

Rapid Transit

Only a hardy variety comedian would risk a trolley-car joke in 1897, for the electric cars were everywhere and indispensable.

Wilmington, Del., had well-moustached motormen who inspired confidence.

Courtesy, American Car and Foundry Company, New York City

Baltimore picnickers took the trolley out to Gwynn Oak Park (right).

Courtesy, The Municipal Museum of the City of Baltimore, Md.

The arrival of the first car in Dearborn, Mich., on Dec. 24, 1897, was quite a civic event. The city fathers gathered to greet the "Special" and be photographed.

Courtesy, Dearborn Historical Commission, Mich.

The Great American Hurry

The picture *below* was taken in 1897 as the Empire State Express was making sixty-four miles an hour.

Harper's Weekly, Mar. 13, 1897
Courtesy, Harper & Brothers, New York City

Courtesy, Scribner Art File

Alexander Winton, a pioneer in the development of the automobile, is seen *above* at the wheel of his 1897 improved model. This car was produced commercially in 1898.

Walt Whitman (deceased 1892) in a comment on the national passion for speed had hoped that provision would be made for an increase in the number of lunatic asylums. Poets are proverbially impractical.

Flood Stage

The latter part of March, 1897, was unseasonably warm and rainy. In three great and distinct waves, flood waters swept down the Mississippi valley, raising the river's level to stages far above the disastrous levels of 1892 and 1893.

Harper's Weekly, Apr. 17, 1897
Courtesy, Harper & Brothers, New York City

The water drowned out the "Bohemian Flats" district of Minneapolis *(left)*.

Homes were hastily abandoned as the river spread wide below St. Paul *(right)*.

Harper's Weekly, Apr. 17, 1897
Courtesy, Harper & Brothers, New York City

Damage was greatest in the Yazoo Delta where ten counties were under water. Greenville, Miss., was isolated on a kind of island preserved by a hastily constructed back-levee *(left)*.

Harper's Weekly, Apr. 24, 1897
Courtesy, Harper & Brothers, New York City

Flood Stage (Continued)

People along the river did what they could, and the President applied to Congress for relief appropriations.

Harper's Bazar, May 8, 1897
Courtesy, Harper's Bazaar, New York City

In the picture *above*, a farmer has rafted all his possessions.

Harper's Bazar, May 8, 1897
Courtesy, Harper's Bazaar, New York City

Stock was herded onto higher ground which might be expected to remain above water.

Down in New Orleans, the river lapped high against the levee at Poland Street (*right*).

Courtesy, Board of Commissioners of the Port of New Orleans, La.

Feeding the World—Wheat

European and Asiatic crop failures had given the wheat and corn farmers of the United States a time of comparative prosperity. Indeed, the rise of farm prices had been a factor in the defeat of William Jennings Bryan.

Courtesy, J. I. Case Company, Racine, Wis.

In the picture *above*, part of the 1897 western wheat crop is being harvested in the old style. Note the horse-power applied to the thrasher through a tumbling-rod.

Scribner's Magazine, November, 1897

Wagons hauled the wheat to the elevators for loading into cars, or for storage against a further rise in price.

At the *right*, a heading reaper is being used on a wheat field in the State of Washington.

Harper's Weekly, July 24, 1897
Courtesy, Harper & Brothers, New York City

Feeding the World—Wheat (*Continued*)

At Pullman, Wash., half a million bushels of wheat awaited shipment in sacks (*right*). Inland waterways were crowded with grain ships (*below*).

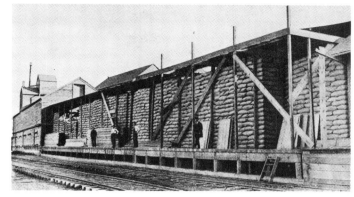

Harper's Weekly, July 24, 1897
Courtesy, Harper & Brothers, New York City

Harper's Weekly, Oct. 9, 1897
Courtesy, Harper & Brothers, New York City

From the giant elevators in Brooklyn, N. Y., the grain spouted into cargo holds for delivery across the ocean.

Harper's Weekly, Oct. 9, 1897
Courtesy, Harper & Brothers, New York City

Feeding the World (*Continued*)

Kansas and Nebraska farmers paid off their mortgages when the crops of 1897 were harvested and sold.

In the picture *left*, one team draws a wagon-train of corn into Manhattan, Kans.

Harper's Weekly, Feb. 12, 1898
Courtesy, Harper & Brothers, New York City

Kansas Valley potatoes found a ready market (*right*).

Harper's Weekly, Sept. 11, 1897
Courtesy, Harper & Brothers, New York City

Through the Kansas City stock-yards (*below*) six million head of livestock passed in 1897.

Harper's Weekly, Sept. 11, 1897. *Courtesy*, Harper & Brothers, New York City

Georgia Peaches

The citizens of Georgia made a determined and successful effort through the Nineties to limit cotton planting and diversify crops. One result of this action was the rise of a profitable trade in peaches.

The yield of large orchards like the one shown *right* was sorted and graded for market in packing-sheds (*below*).

Harper's Weekly, July 10, 1897
Courtesy, Harper & Brothers, New York City

Harper's Weekly, July 10, 1897
Courtesy, Harper & Brothers, New York City

But the popular northern idea of the "New South" was still limited to the picturesque and archaic sides of its life. The 1897 sketch of a wagon yard *right* was what the public wanted.

Harper's Bazar, Oct. 23, 1897
Courtesy, Harper's Bazaar, New York City

Timber

Heedless and wasteful commercial exploitation was depleting national forest resources to the point where outcries of "Conservationists" began to be heeded in high places. There was no need for Paul Bunyan and Babe the Blue Ox to snake whole sections down to the sawmills. Mere lumberjacks were doing it very nicely.

In northern Minnesota the logs piled up at the landing.

The log train *right* was photographed at Walker, Minn. Taking the logs out by rail was a comparative innovation in the Nineties.

But despite all technological changes in the industry, the lumberjacks remained tough, reckless and productive of legends. In the picture *left*, they are gathered at the "Wannagan," on pay-day.

All illustrations on this page are by the *courtesy* of the Minnesota Historical Society, St. Paul

Timber *(Continued)*

Life in the lumber camps was not for the weak or the sensitive.

Handling the tote-team *right* with its load of supplies on a sledge was not a leisured job.

The blacksmith *(left)* would be kept busy.

Bored men in barracks have always cherished pin-up girls.

All illustrations on this page are by the *courtesy* of the Minnesota Historical Society, St. Paul

Developing Seaports

Favorably situated southern and northwestern port cities were quick to see opportunity in newly-developing trades and trade-routes.

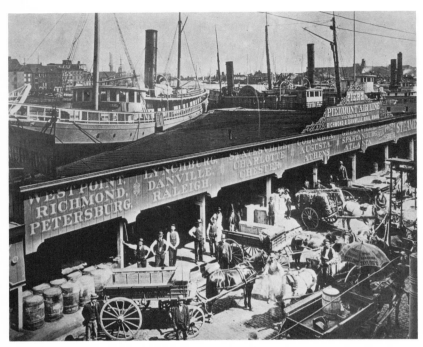

Baltimore challenged New York's supremacy in ocean trade and did not neglect the local traffic advertised *left*.

Courtesy, The Municipal Museum of the City of Baltimore, Md.

The advantages of the Port of New Orleans in the trade to the east coast of South America attracted new business to that ancient and pleasant city.

Courtesy, Board of Commissioners of the Port of New Orleans, La.

Below is shown a view of Seattle, Wash., in the summer of 1897.

Harper's Weekly, Nov. 13, 1897. *Courtesy,* Harper & Brothers, New York City

On June 17, 1897, the *Portland* arrived in Seattle with a cargo of Alaskan miners and gold-dust. The Klondike boom that followed gave Seattle an opportunity to diversify her lumber export trade and so prosper.

Klondike

Not since the first news from California, almost fifty years earlier, had a gold discovery aroused such excitement. The event had more significance than the public suspected, however; for this increase in gold production, added to the additional yield from low-grade ore made possible by the Cyanide Process, destroyed the validity of Bryan's Free Silver argument and made the "Sound Money" cry less grievous in the ears of labor and the farmer.

Even while prospective million-aires were streaming out of Forty Mile Post in Alaska (*right*) to stake their claims, advertisements like the one *below* were appearing in the press.

Harper's Weekly, Aug. 7, 1897
Courtesy, Harper & Brothers, New York City

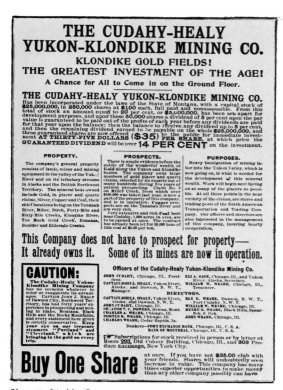

Harper's Weekly, Sept. 11, 1897
Courtesy, Harper & Brothers, New York City

Miners left by boat from Juneau for the start of the adventure and headed for the upper tributaries of the Yukon by way of Chilkoot Pass (*right*) on foot or sledge.

Harper's Weekly, July 31, 1897
Courtesy, Harper & Brothers, New York City

Florida

At the opposite extreme of national geography and temperature, Henry M. Flagler was putting gold into the east coast of Florida, combining existing railroads and building new ones to further his dream of an "American Riviera." He had scored successes with luxury hotels at St. Augustine and Palm Beach. Now he began to extend the rails far south to Miami.

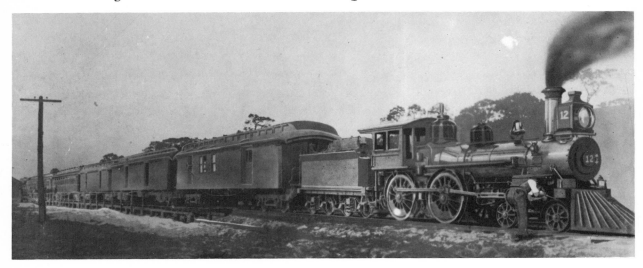

The wood-burning engine *above* pulled the first passenger train into Miami—Apr. 22, 1896.

East Flagler Street and Biscayne Boulevard, Miami, is shown *below* as it looked in the late Nineties.

All illustrations on this page are by the *courtesy* of the Florida East Coast Railway Company, St. Augustine, **Fla.**

Gotham

As you looked south down Fifth Avenue from 35th Street in 1898, the New York Club and A. T. Stewart's original "marble palace" sandwiched a small business building; and the thirteen stories of the old Waldorf-Astoria towered in the background.

Courtesy, The Waldorf-Astoria, New York City

Uptown, the piers of the Cathedral of St. John the Divine were rising over Morningside Avenue.

Courtesy, The J. Clarence Davies Collection, Museum of the City of New York

On Apr. 27, 1897, the remains of Ulysses S. Grant were formally laid away in an imposing tomb on Riverside Drive.

The military procession is shown *right* arriving for the ceremony.

Courtesy, Museum of the City of New York

"Remember the Maine"

Since 1895, the people of Cuba had been in active rebellion against the rule of Spain. Atrocity stories, true or false, were liberally featured in the United States press, and aroused humanitarians to call for intervention. Business men looked forward to extension of trade should Spanish authority be succeeded by a Cuban republic presumably grateful for our help. Strategists of the Mahan school considered control of Cuba essential to domination over the Caribbean Sea. The "Cuerpo de Consejo" of the Cuban Revolutionary Party (commonly called the "Junta") is shown *below*. This group operated in New York as a fund-raising body and as recruiters of filibusters. Owners of sugar estates had to buy immunity from crop-burning from both Spaniards and Cuban patriots.

Courtesy, Anuario Bibliografico Cubano, Havana

Late in January, 1898, the *U. S. S. Maine* entered the harbor of Havana for a courtesy call, as shown *below*.

At about 9:40 P. M. on the evening of February 15, a dull explosion forward, followed by a much more powerful blast, sent parts of the *Maine* high in the air. The after part of the ship sank slowly. Two hundred and sixty men were lost. The question whether an external mine or an internal explosion caused the disaster was never answered and never will be, since we towed the hulk to sea and sank it.

Courtesy, Scribner Art File

War With Spain

Under pressure of all kinds, President McKinley dropped negotiations for a peaceful settlement of Cuban questions, including the "*Maine*" incident, and yielded to popular hysteria. On April 11 he sent a war message to Congress.

All over the nation, men flocked to recruiting stations. The last traces of bitterness over the Civil War disappeared in martial enthusiasm to free Cuba, and Joe Wheeler and Fitzhugh Lee put on again the blue uniform.

Harper's Weekly, Mar. 26, 1898
Courtesy, Harper & Brothers, New York City

"Fire When Ready, Gridley"

The U. S. Pacific squadron, already in Asiatic waters, headed for the Philippine Islands, Spain's rich possession in the Far East.

Harper's Weekly, June 25, 1898. Courtesy, Harper & Brothers, New York City

On May 1, 1898, one week after the declaration of war, Admiral Dewey on the *Olympia* led the Pacific squadron into Manila Bay, P. I., sank all ten vessels in the Spanish Admiral Montojo's fleet and silenced the shore batteries. The picture *above* was drawn from a sketch made on the spot.

Call to Arms

The immediate objective of the armed forces was the island of Cuba. The Regular Army, small but well-trained, presented no problems. The hundreds of thousands of volunteers, however, were equipped mainly with enthusiasm. Old Springfield rifles were their arms when they had any on arrival at ports of embarkation. But they came streaming in.

Courtesy, Wyoming State Library and State Historical Department, Cheyenne

At the *left* a cavalry unit is seen leaving Cheyenne, Wyo.

Tampa, Fla., was the scene of hasty training maneuvers as shown *right*.

Harper's Weekly, May 28, 1898
Courtesy, Harper & Brothers, New York City

Harper's Weekly, May 28, 1898
Courtesy, Harper & Brothers, New York City

Nine miles away, commandeered transports of all kinds waited at Port Tampa, an embarkation point chosen apparently for its inaccessibility and lack of facilities.

The waiting men sickened on "embalmed beef" and sweltered in heavy "blues" under the Florida sun. Khaki cloth could not be provided.

The Rough Riders

Colorful, unconventional and enthusiastic, this volunteer cavalry outfit reflected the temperament of its Lieutenant-Colonel. Theodore Roosevelt had resigned his place on the Board of Naval Strategy to Capt. A. T. Mahan and joined with Col. Leonard Wood in command of the Rough Riders. A view of the picket line at their Texas training camp is seen *below*.

Harper's Weekly, June 4, 1898. *Courtesy*, Harper & Brothers, New York City

Scribner's Magazine, January, 1899

Recruits from the cattle-ranges and mining camps found little difficulty in the camp chore pictured *above*.

The amenities were not forgotten. In the picture of the Officers' Mess *left*, Col. Wood and Lt.-Col. Roosevelt sit at the head of the table.

Courtesy, Scribner Art File

Santiago Blockaded

News had come, meanwhile, that a Spanish cruiser squadron under Admiral Cervera had sailed from the Cape Verde Islands. The resultant howls for protection from seaboard American cities subsided when it became known that the Spanish ships had anchored in land-locked Santiago Bay on May 19. The portion of our Atlantic Fleet in Cuban waters immediately set up a blockade.

Events of the next few weeks provided a war-correspondent's field day. From descriptions received, an artist produced the sketch *left* of Richmond P. Hobson and his men scuttling the old collier *Merrimac* in the bottle-neck entrance of Santiago Bay on the south-east coast of Cuba early in the morning of June 3.

Harper's Weekly, June 18, 1898. *Courtesy,* Harper & Brothers, New York City

Harper's Weekly, June 25, 1898. *Courtesy,* Harper & Brothers, New York City

Meanwhile, at Port Tampa, a disorganized Commissary labored to get an expeditionary force of eighteen thousand men off to Cuba.

Invasion

Gen. Shafter's army put off from Port Tampa on June 15. Behind them, they left a host of sick men, a hopeless confusion and the mounts for the Rough Riders. *Below* is shown a part of the landing at Daiquiri, made without opposition between the twentieth and the twenty-fifth of June. The Spanish Captain-General seemed strangely unconcerned and mustered only a handful of his available troops to block the movement toward the high ground around Santiago.

Harper's Weekly, July 16, 1898
Courtesy, Harper & Brothers, New York City

Harper's Weekly, July 30, 1898
Courtesy, Harper & Brothers, New York City

The troops pressed forward through tropical vegetation and swampy ground (*left*). An engagement took place at Las Guasimas as the Spanish outposts were driven in.

San Juan Hill was the key point directly blocking the American advance: El Caney opposed the enveloping operation of our right wing.

On July 1, Lawton's division carried El Caney. In a simultaneous attack, Kent's division, including the (unhorsed) Rough Riders, charged up San Juan Hill. To the *right* is seen one of the few authentic pictures of the charge of the Rough Riders.

Courtesy, Scribner Art File

Santiago

In possession of the hills around Santiago, the United States Army began siege operations. Admiral Cervera was persuaded to escape before the city fell and his ships could be taken at anchor. At nine in the morning, July 3, 1898, the Spanish squadron made its best speed out of the harbor and headed westward. The blockading squadron of battleships and cruisers closed in and gave chase.

By one o'clock the Spanish ships had been overtaken and destroyed. To the *left* is the wreck of Cervera's flagship, *Infanta Maria Teresa*, as sketched on the spot by Carlton Chapman.

Harper's Weekly, July 30, 1898
Courtesy, Harper & Brothers, New York City

At the *right* is shown the hulk of the cruiser *Reina Mercedes*, sunk attempting a sortie on the night of July 4.

Courtesy, The National Archives, Washington, D. C.

The captain of the Spanish warship *Cristobal Colon* is seen at the *left*, as he checks off the names of his crew at the prison camp.

Harper's Weekly, July 23, 1898
Courtesy, Harper & Brothers, New York City

Spreading the News

Newspaper correspondents reported the war news as if they were dealing with a sports event. One of the most glamorous of these correspondents was Richard Harding Davis (*right*)—a prominent writer of fiction and supposedly the model for one of the variants of the "Gibson Man" (see page 93).

Artist-correspondents were attached to the Fleet, and one of them drew the sketch *below*, of the *Oregon* and the *Texas* in pursuit of the *Vizcaya* at the battle of Santiago Bay.

Courtesy, Scribner Art File

Harper's Weekly, July 30, 1898
Courtesy, Harper & Brothers, New York City

Currier and Ives, in the last years of their activity, circulated the naval print shown *below.*

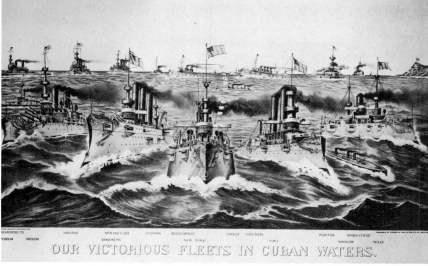

OUR VICTORIOUS FLEETS IN CUBAN WATERS.

Courtesy, Robert Fridenberg Galleries, New York City

Manila Again

Ever since the sinking of Montojo's ships in May, Admiral Dewey had been blockading the harbor of Manila, warding off German gestures of sympathy with Spain, and temporizing with Filipino insurgents under Aguinaldo. On July 17, the first troop transports arrived and Cavite was occupied.

By July 31, Gen. Wesley Merritt considered himself strong enough to invest the city of Manila, and began to negotiate with the Spanish garrison.

By arrangement with the Spanish authorities, the Spanish positions were surrendered in such a manner that Aguinaldo and his adherents were unable to make a joint occupation of the city with our troops. The insurgent leader (shown *left* with his chief supporters) was outraged.

Harper's Weekly, Nov. 12, 1898
Courtesy, Harper & Brothers, New York City

At the *right* the American flag is seen as it was hoisted over the Spanish citadel by Lt.-Col. McCoy of the 1st Colorado Volunteers.

Harper's Weekly, Oct. 15, 1898
Courtesy, Harper & Brothers, New York City

Gen. Merritt was in a touchy situation. He had 8,500 men to hold a city of 300,000 people, to guard 13,000 Spanish prisoners and to fend off at least 10,000 angry Filipino insurgents.

Aguinaldo, elected provisional President of the Visayan Republic, moved his government to Malolos. The end was not yet. In Manila, hungry Filipinos flocked for rations to the Army's Commissary (*left*).

Harper's Weekly, Nov. 12, 1898
Courtesy, Harper & Brothers, New York City

Paths of Glory

Soldiers and sailors returned to taste the sweets of victory at home. Local celebrations were held to welcome them.

In the Naval Parade at New York, the *Oregon* (*right*) attracted great attention for her record run around Cape Horn to be present at the destruction of Cervera's squadron.

Harper's Weekly, Sept. 3, 1898
Courtesy, Harper & Brothers, New York City

Harper's Weekly, Nov. 5, 1898
Courtesy, Harper & Brothers, New York City

One of the great moments at the Peace Jubilee in Philadelphia was the passage of Lt. Hobson and his crew through the court of honor (*left*).

Meanwhile at Camp Wikoff, Long Island, thousands of fever victims were held in strict quarantine. Each returning transport or hospital ship contributed its share to the ambulance trains headed for Montauk Point *below*.

Harper's Weekly, Aug. 27, 1898
Courtesy, Harper & Brothers, New York City

4

THE FULL DINNER PAIL

The average citizen of the United States accepted his involvement in colonial problems without much protest. As a result of the war, although opinion had been much divided as to its necessity or justice, a general business boom had come. The money market seemed stable once and for all; at the end of the century (did it end in 1899 or 1900?), peace and prosperity seemed to have returned.

Courtesy, Mr. Myron F. Henkel, Springfield, Ill

When the Wild West Show came to Springfield, Ill., a new attraction rode in the parade—a group of genuine Rough Riders (*left*).

The small-town man cherished his lodge membership. At the *right*, the Odd Fellows of El Campo, Tex., parade behind their band.

Courtesy, The Library of the University of Texas, Austin

Once one of the most potent forces in American politics, the Grand Army of the Republic dressed its lines to parade past Philadelphia's City Hall.

Harper's Weekly, Sept. 16, 1899. Courtesy, Harper & Brothers, New York City

Dances

On every level of society, dancing was a favorite diversion. The day of the "spieler" had departed and a more genteel effect was aimed at in the ballroom.

The young ladies of Goucher College, Baltimore, Md., shown *right* were practicing a figure with a proper sense of its importance.

Courtesy, The Baltimore Sun and Enoch Pratt Free Library, Baltimore, Md.

Dances had their function as fund-raisers for worthy causes. Note the emphasis on the music in the poster to the *left*.

Courtesy, San Mateo County Historical Association, San Mateo, Calif.

Courtesy, The Valentine Museum, Richmond, Va.

Above is shown an interval of the Easter German at Richmond, Va.

Social Rites

Certain kinds of entertainment were still distinctly formal in character.

The début introduced a young girl into the society of her family's friends. In 1899 a débutante appeared with comparatively little fanfare, as shown *left*.

Afternoon tea had a protocol of its own. *Below*.

Harper's Bazar, Dec. 2, 1899. Courtesy, Harper's Bazaar, New York City

Alexander Black, *Miss America*. 1898

Courtesy, Mr. Myron F. Henkel, Springfield, Ill.

An engagement was announced at the somewhat self-conscious party shown *above*.

Lost Inhibitions

Animal spirits were given play at definite places and seasons.

Through St. Charles Street, New Orleans, the King of the Mardi Gras passed in state (*right*), inaugurating his brief but lusty reign.

Harper's Weekly, Mar. 4, 1899
Courtesy, Harper & Brothers, New York City

Courtesy, Mr. Paul Boyton,
Sheepshead Bay, N. Y.

Coney Island welcomed a new and sensational "ride," the Shoot the Chutes, advertised *left* and seen in its first season *below*.

A troupe of swimmers and divers performed in the pool when the chutes were not shooting.

Courtesy, Mr. Paul Boyton, Sheepshead Bay, N. Y.

Gittie Up

Courtesy, The Hempstead Library, Hempstead, N. Y.

The runabout used for ordinary driving was much the same whether (as in the picture of two Long Island speed demons *above*) you were going to the village for the mail, or taking a brief turn around the Park as the Richmond, Va., lady shown *below* has just done.

Courtesy, The Valentine Museum, Richmond, Va.

The Brewer's Big Horses

The fight against the saloon and all it implied was opposed in the cities by the influence of politician-saloon-keepers. The establishment at the *right* belonged to the famous Alderman of Chicago's First Ward, Mr. "Hinky-Dink" Mike Kenna.

Courtesy, The Managing Editor

Outside the large cities the forces of temperance had greater victories. "Drinks" advertised for sale at the Michigan camp-meeting refreshment tent shown *left* would be lemonade and "phosphates" or bottled soda-water.

Harper's Weekly, July 22, 1899
Courtesy, Harper & Brothers,
New York City

Militant prohibitionists attended the rally in the main square of Nacogdoches, Tex., seen at the *right*. The largest banner reads, "Save Our Boys."

Courtesy, The Library of the University of Texas, Austin

Fashion Notes: End of a Century

The task of the *modiste* had become complicated by the existence of two different kinds of woman—the "New" and the conventional.

Alexander Black, *Miss America*. 1898

The conventional lady's garments were designed to set off her essential womanliness as in the picture to the *left* and suited traditional feminine attitudes.

The picture *below, left,* shows a décor of ostrich plumes, feather boa and chatelaine, a little overdone but true to the concept of a "womanly woman."

Alexander Black, *Miss America*. 1898

The veil shown in the picture *above* was ideal for cute tricks such as freeing the end of the nose by a pout, or tugging gracefully at the lower hem to display the fineness of a hand.

Courtesy, Nevada State Historical Society, Reno

Fashion Notes (*Continued*)

Thoughtless people might scoff at the "new woman's" aspirations, but the designers and manufacturers of clothing clambered on the band wagon.

A coming generation which engaged in athletic activities like that shown at the *right* would want the product advertised *below*.

Courtesy, Public Relations Office, University of Nebraska, Lincoln

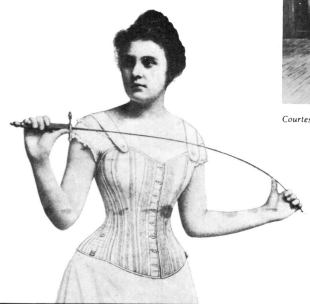

Physical Perfection

can never be attained in a rigid corset. The growing girl or matured woman who desires physical beauty find FERRIS' GOOD SENSE CORSET WAIST the ideal garment. It is the only waist that creates the perfection of contour demanded by particular women, without the slightest restricting or discomfort. Thousands of women are wearing

FERRIS' Good Sense Corset Waist

If you would like to know how they look and fit, we will send you a book of photographic pictures, free.
FERRIS' GOOD SENSE CORSET WAISTS are **sold by all leading retailers.** Do not substitutes. Ladies', $1.00 to $2.75; Misses', 50 cents to $1.00; Children's, 25 cents to 50 c
Made only by THE FERRIS BROS. CO., 341 Broadway, New York.

Courtesy, N. W. Ayer & Son, Inc., Philadelphia, Pa.

By popular demand, the traditional man's "boater" straw has been feminized. *Below*.

Harper's Bazar, Feb. 10, 1900
Courtesy, Harper's Bazaar, New York City

LADIES STRAW SAILORS
1899
SHAPES NOW READY
$4.00
$5.00
$4.00
KNOX HATS
All mail orders promptly executed. Send for 1899 Catalogue
KNOX-HATTER 194 FIFTH AVE. N.Y.
FIFTH AVENUE HOTEL

Harper's Weekly, Mar. 4, 1899
Courtesy, Harper & Brothers, New York City

Displayed *left*, the Cuban heel was introduced that same season of 1899 as a boon to the "outdoor girl."

Gratitude of the Republic

When Admiral George Dewey returned to the United States, his mission completed some seventeen months after the victory of Manila Bay, the American public released on him all its pent-up love of lionizing. He received a series of welcomes that rivaled the triumphs of Rome.

Courtesy, Scribner Art File

The *Olympia*, at the head of the squadron, was sighted off Sandy Hook on Tuesday, Sept. 26, 1899. Gov. Roosevelt and other notables went aboard the flagship to extend an official greeting *(left)*.

A triumphal arch *(right)* had been erected at the southern end of Madison Square, and symbolized "Naval Victory."

Harper's Weekly, Oct. 7, 1899
Courtesy, Harper & Brothers, New York City

But an unthinking bluntness and a naive honesty disqualified the Admiral as a popular heroic figure. After the parades and the shouting were over, he refused to hold the pose. The Washington, D. C., house shown *left* had been given to him by popular subscription. He was genuinely puzzled when press and public gave tongue over his presentation of the deed to his newly-wedded wife.

Harper's Weekly, Nov. 4, 1899
Courtesy, Harper & Brothers, New York City

Again Manila

The clash of cymbals and the thump of big drums at countless parades in honor of the returned Admiral did not quite drown out the crackle of rifle fire from across the Pacific. Filipino insurgents did not propose to exchange Spanish rule for American.

Early in February, 1899, a revolt was put down by house-to-house fighting (*right*). A part of Manila was badly damaged by fire, as seen in the panoramic view *below*.

Harper's Weekly, Apr. 22, 1899
Courtesy, Harper & Brothers, New York City

Harper's Weekly, Apr. 22, 1899. Courtesy, Harper & Brothers, New York City

Gen. Arthur MacArthur (*right*), in command of an offensive against insurgent forces north of Manila, captured the provisional capital of Malolos and dispersed Aguinaldo's army, but that leader retreated into the woods and fought a tough guerrilla war until Gen. Funston captured him in March, 1901.

Harper's Weekly, May 27, 1899
Courtesy, Harper & Brothers, New York City

Suburbs

In greater numbers, people who could afford it were shifting their homes outside the cities in search of quiet, fresh air and space. At the home shown *below*, near Richmond, Va., there was plenty of room on the wide lawn for the boys and their bicycles, the smaller children and their goat-cart.

Courtesy, The Valentine Museum, Richmond, Va.

Behind less pretentious suburban houses, the "back yard" was a place for play, for relaxation and family entertainment.

Courtesy, Mrs. Frank Ewing, Grand Rapids, Mich.

Parlors

Every house had one room at least where the family put its best foot forward and displayed what treasures it possessed.

The parlor *right* was in a spacious and comfortable Lincoln, Neb., home. Note the square piano, the framed steel-engraving on the wall, the ornate oil lamp. The library or "den" may be seen just through the doorway.

Courtesy, Nebraska State Historical Society, Lincoln

Less money was spent on the room *left*, and a less formal effect produced. This Lincoln, Neb., parlor has an upright piano, the lamp is not so heavily ornamented and the top of the piano has been humanized by a few family photographs and a vase of cat-tails.

Courtesy, Nebraska State Historical Society, Lincoln

The parlor in the Cooper County, Mo., farm house shown *right* was an all-purpose room.

Courtesy, Charles van Ravenswaay Collection, Missouri Historical Society, St. Louis

Education

These years saw a continuous adaptation of educational practice to meet new challenges.

Courtesy, Atlanta University, Ga.

In the South, Atlanta University stressed both the practical and the cultural sides of life in the higher education it offered to negro boys and girls. A class in Greek is shown reciting.

At the *right* is a class in fine sewing at Atlanta University.

Courtesy, Atlanta University, Ga.

In New York, and other crowded urban areas, Vacation Schools had proved themselves valuable factors in reducing summer delinquency. The boys shown at the *left* were learning to model in clay.

Harper's Bazar, Aug. 19, 1899. *Courtesy,* Harper's Bazaar, New York City

Sport Talk

Paced by a Long Island Railroad locomotive, Charles M. Murphy rode a mile in sixty-five seconds on a bicycle, thus becoming immortal as "Mile-a-Minute Murphy."

At the *left* is shown the hero ready for the trial on June 21, 1899. The feat itself is seen at the *right*, as Murphy pedals down the specially constructed board track.

Harper's Weekly, July 8, 1899. *Courtesy*, Harper & Brothers, New York City

Later that summer, the first of Sir Thomas Lipton's *Shamrocks*, challenger for the *America's* Cup, was defeated by the American defender, *Columbia*.

In the picture *right*, *Columbia* is leading as the yachts bear down to the starting line.

Harper's Weekly, Oct. 21, 1899
Courtesy, Harper & Brothers, New York City

Science a Servant

As engineers applied the lore of the laboratory to practical matters, an era of easeful living appeared certain to open with the new century.

Harper's Weekly, Aug. 18, 1900. *Courtesy*, Harper & Brothers, New York City

New York City's problem of water supply was about to be solved by the new Croton Dam, seen *above* in the construction stage.

Harper's Weekly, Mar. 31, 1900
Courtesy, Harper & Brothers, New York City

Mr. Edison has perfected the Phonograph

This is the Instrument

THE EDISON "CONCERT" PHONOGRAPH

It perfectly reproduces the human voice — JUST AS LOUD — just as clear — just as sweet.

It duplicates instrumental music with pure-toned brilliance and satisfying intensity. Used with Edison Concert Records, its reproduction is free from all mechanical noises. Only the music or the voice is heard.

It is strong and vibrant enough to fill the largest auditorium. It is smooth and broad enough for the parlor.

The highest type of talking-machine ever before produced bears no comparison with the Edison Concert Phonograph. The price is $125.

Full particulars can be obtained from all dealers in Phonographs; or by addressing The National Phonograph Co., New York, asking for Concert Catalogue No. 36.

Six other styles of Phonographs, including the Edison Gem, price $7.50.

NONE GENUINE WITHOUT THIS   TRADE MARK

Thomas A. Edison

Harper's Weekly, May 13, 1899
Courtesy, Harper & Brothers, New York City

On Mar. 24, 1900, the crowd shown *above*, in New York's City Hall Park, watched the breaking of ground for the new Subway

The 1899 advertisement at the *left* spoke for itself.

Wireless

In the spring of 1899, the Army ran a few experiments in practical field use of Hertzian oscillators.

The picture *right* was taken on the roof of the War Department building, as a message was being transmitted to the field receiving outfit.

Harper's Weekly, May 13, 1899
Courtesy, Harper & Brothers, New York City

Later in that year, the Navy tried out the new Marconi system in successful communication up to nine miles distance between the battleships *Massachusetts* and *New York.* Marconi is seen *left* at the "grasshopper" key of the transmitter aboard the *New York.*

Harper's Weekly, Nov. 11, 1899
Courtesy, Harper & Brothers, New York City

On Nov. 15, 1899, the newspaper reproduced at the *right* was sold aboard the United States liner *St. Paul,* the first publication of shipboard news by wireless ever attempted.

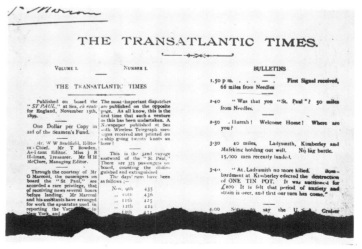

Courtesy, Radio Corporation of America, New York City

Motor Cars

Harper's Bazar, Sept. 23, 1899
Courtesy, Harper's Bazaar, New York City

For the first automobile parade ever held, at Newport, R. I., Sept. 7, 1899, Mrs. Astor (shown *left*) decked her entry in trappings that even an Astor horse might envy.

Advertising of new cars made no extravagant claims. Note in the specimen *right* the cost for a hundred mile drive.

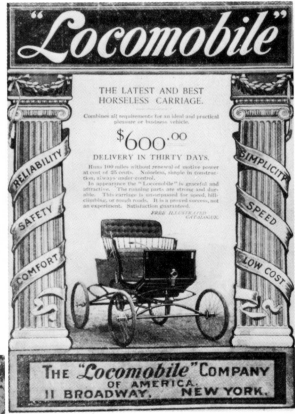

Harper's Weekly, Aug. 26, 1899
Courtesy, Harper & Brothers, New York City

Harper's Weekly, Oct. 21, 1899
Courtesy, Harper & Brothers, New York City

The imported De Dion motorcycle shown *left* was highly recommended. "With slight assistance from the pedals it will mount a fifteen percent grade."

Motor Cars *(Continued)*

In the fall of 1900, the galleries of New York's Madison Square Garden looked down on something new—an Automobile Show.

Harper's Weekly, Nov. 17, 1900. *Courtesy,* Harper & Brothers, New York City

Courtesy, Scribner Art File

The father of a family is trying the controls of one of the Show exhibits in the picture to the *left* as a salesman stands hopefully by.

The first Mack Truck was a bus—the 1900 vehicle seen at the *right.*

Courtesy, Mack-International Motor Truck Corporation, New York City

Farm Machinery

By the year 1900, production of wheat and corn was about double what it had been in 1870. A factor in this increased yield was the widespread use of steam power on the farms. Larger acreages could be planted and harvested.

Courtesy, J. I. Case Company, Racine, Wis.

Above and to the *right* are seen stages in the building of traction engines. Note the purposeful pose of the apprentice at left center in the picture *above*.

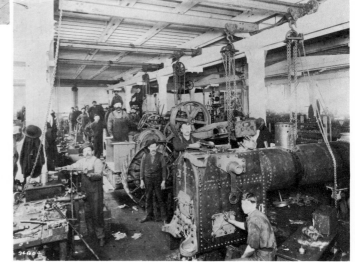

Courtesy, J. I. Case Company, Racine, Wis.

The picture to the *left*, made in 1900, shows one of the first applications of a caterpillar drive to a farm engine.

Courtesy, Scribner Art File

Steel

Just before the turn of the century, the turbulent American steel industry successfully entered the world export market and filled foreign iron-masters with alarm.

In the vast ore-yards of the Illinois Company's South Works (*right*), the steam shovel was used to load the charging buggies.

Courtesy, United States Steel Corporation, New York City

At the Bellaire Works, the hungry blast furnaces were charged from hand barrows (*left*).

Courtesy, United States Steel Corporation,
New York City

At night the glare of the Duquesne Works (*right*) lit the smoky sky.

Harper's Weekly, Apr. 21, 1900
Courtesy, Harper & Brothers, New York City

Zinc

A rise in the price of zinc ore to over thirty dollars a ton brought a sudden boom to northern Arkansas where rich deposits lay in the stratified flanks of the Ozarks.

From the town of Yellville, Ark. (*left*), the ore was freighted down the White River to the railroad, and thence by rail and sea to Belgium for reduction into metal.

The mine whose entrance is shown *right* was near Buffalo City, Ark.

Ore was crushed and separated, at the mill seen to the *left*.

The Nation's Food

A traction engine is shown *right* driving a thrashing machine, as the wheat harvest of 1900 went to market.

Courtesy, J. I. Case Company, Racine, Wis.

Courtesy, H. J. Heinz Company, Pittsburgh, Pa.

The men at the *left* are sorting horse-radish roots on a large commercial farm.

Part of the 1900 crop of oranges is being packed for shipment at this Redlands, Calif., plant.

Courtesy, The Edison Institute, Dearborn, Mich.

The Nation's Food *(Continued)*

Courtesy, The Valentine Museum, Richmond, Va.

Garden truck for the day-by-day needs of the cities found its way to produce-markets. The picture *left* shows the market at Franklin and Eighteenth Streets, Richmond, Va.

Beside the Bayou Teche in Louisiana, sugar cane was fed into the rolling jaws of the crusher pictured at the *right.*

Harper's Weekly, Apr. 14, 1900
Courtesy, Harper & Brothers, New York City

The warehouses alongside the piers at Brooklyn, N. Y., were filled with coffee, neatly classified by mark and chop.

W. H. Ukers, *All About Coffee.* 1935. Courtesy, The Tea and Coffee Trade Journal, New York City

The Retail Store

The typical "corner grocery" shown *right* was in a suburb of Chicago.

Courtesy, Chicago Lawn Historical Society and Chicago Public Library, Ill.

Beer steins were prominently displayed in the stock of this Lincoln, Neb., jewelry shop.

Courtesy, Nebraska State Historical Society, Lincoln

The prosperous shoe store shown *right* was at 512 East Adams Street, Springfield, Ill.

Courtesy, Mr. Myron F. Henkel, Springfield, Ill.

The Retail Store *(Continued)*

Courtesy, The Great Atlantic and Pacific Tea Company, New York City

The chain stores continued to flourish. As yet they had not expanded their stocks much beyond teas and coffees. The helmeted policeman in the picture *left* was presumably a customer.

The milkman and his patient horse were familiar figures.

Grocery prices on the list *below* should interest the modern housewife.

Courtesy, Ravenswood-Lake View Historical Association, sponsored by The Chicago Public Library, Ill.

Don't throw this Circular away

Until you have read it—it will Save you Money and Time....

Fresh Bread, 2 loaves for.... 5c	Ground Pepper, Cinnamon, All-
Soda Crackers, per pound...... 5c	spice, Cloves, Mustard, per lb.18c
Bremner Soda Crackers, pkg... 7c	Brown sugar, per lb............ 5c
Uneeda Biscuits, per pkg...... 4½c	Granulated sugar............. 6c
Bird Seed 10c	Powdered or Frosting sugar... 7c
Red Cross brand Macaroni..... 7c	Cut loaf sugar................ 7c
Pancake Flour............... 8c	Pumpkin per can.............. 8c
Sapolio, per cake............. 7c	Paris Sweet Corn 10c
Scourene..................... 4c	Lakeside early June Peas......10c
Scrubine..................... 4c	Bartlett Pears................12c
Amber soap, 7 bars for.......25c	Boston Baked Beans.......... 5c
Scotch Family soap, 6 bars ...25c	Pine Apple.................12½c
Armour's White soap, per bar.. 4c	Sweet Potatoes............... 9c
Armour's Tar soap, per bar.... 4c	Cocoa.......................10c
Armour's Washing Powder.... 4c	¼ lb can Price's baking powder.21c
Wheatall, per pkg 9c	1lb can Baking powder........13c
Vitos........................12c	25c bottle Vanilla Extract.....20c
Ralston breakfast food..,......12c	Pure Salad Oil, per bottle......25c
Shredded Wheat biscuit........11c	Heinz's Strawberry Preserves,
Quaker Oats.................. 8c	per pound 15c
Nutflake Oatmeal............. 8c	Potash or Lye, with patent
13 lbs Oatmeal................25c	covers, per can.............15c
5 lbs white or yellow Cornmeal.. 5c	Oil, 5 gallons.................50c
Gasoline, 5 gallons............50c	

These goods are Standard goods, and we will be glad to show you other goods at the same margins but not quoted on this circular.
Respectfully,

E. E. SCHLIESKE
CASH GROCER

Courtesy, Chicago Lawn Historical Society and Chicago Public Library, Ill.

Courtesy, National Biscuit Company, New York City

Above is shown the 1900 Uneeda Biscuit box, a pioneer experiment in packaging and retail trade promotion.

Disasters

Despite general progress and prosperity, there were always local disasters to oppress the too soaring spirit of man.

Courtesy, The Essex Institute, Salem, Mass.

On Mar. 26, 1899, the steamer *Norseman* went ashore on Tom Moore's Rocks off Marblehead, Mass.

The spring freshet shown *right* swamped lower Main Street in Richmond, Va.

Courtesy, The Valentine Museum, Richmond, Va.

The chemical warehouse of Tarrant and Company burned and exploded, taking the lives of several New York firemen and wrecking the Greenwich Street Elevated Railroad.

Harper's Weekly, Nov. 3, 1900
Courtesy, Harper & Brothers, New York City

Galveston Flood

Galveston, Tex., stood on the northeasterly end of an island off the Texas coast at an elevation of about ten feet above the sea. At ten in the morning of Sept. 8, 1900, a gale was blowing over Galveston; by noon, the wind was at hurricane force and great waves were pounding over the summer pavilions at the beach; at three in the afternoon, the barometer stood at 29. Then a full tropical hurricane struck the city, with the waters of the Gulf flooding in to a depth of eight feet and a wind registering ninety-six miles an hour before the Weather Bureau was wrecked. By midnight the storm was over. More than five thousand lives had been lost.

Harper's Weekly, Sept. 29, 1900. *Courtesy*, Harper & Brothers, New York City

Residential districts were reduced to kindling (*above*).

Harper's Weekly, Sept. 29, 1900
Courtesy, Harper & Brothers, New York City

The storm destroyed the shops along Tremont Street (*left*) and among other public buildings the Orphan Asylum (*below*).

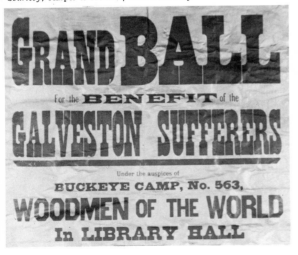

Courtesy, San Mateo County Historical Association, San Mateo, Calif.

Typical of the sympathetic reaction of the whole nation was the poster at the *left*.

Yellow Fever

A commission of Army medical officers, headed by Dr. Walter Reed, was appointed to search out the cause and means of transmission of the disease after an outbreak among United States soldiers at Havana. In the fall of 1900, building on the researches of Doctors Finlay and Carter, Dr. Reed and his associates proved that the bite of the Aëdes Aegypti mosquito transmitted the virus of yellow fever.

At the *right* is a portrait of Dr. Jesse W. Lazear, a member of the Commission, who was the first to die in controlled experiments on human subjects. He died on Sept. 18, 1900, after being bitten by a mosquito previously infected.

U. S. Senate, Executive Document No. 822, 61st Congress, 3rd Session

Courtesy, Scribner Art File

Below is shown the female mosquito, transmitter of a disease that had ravaged port cities for centuries.

The theory was worked out conclusively on an oddly assorted group of volunteers and hired men in quarantined Camp Lazear (*above*), near a suburb of Havana.

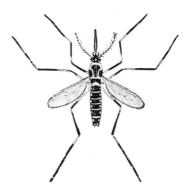

U. S. Senate, Executive Document No. 822, 61st Congress, 3rd Session

Coal Strike

Toward the end of summer, 1900, the anthracite miners struck for a ten percent increase in wages.

The mass meeting *left* was held at Scranton, Pa.

Harper's Weekly, Sept. 29, 1900
Courtesy, Harper & Brothers, New York City

The strikers dramatized their protest by parades, like the one in Mahanoy City, Pa., shown *right*.

Harper's Weekly, Oct. 6, 1900
Courtesy, Harper & Brothers, New York City

John Mitchell and his fellow officers of the United Mine Workers (*left*) fought a successful strike. They were aided, perhaps, by Mark Hanna's reminder to the mine owners that it was an election year, and a ten percent raise might be less expensive to them than Mr. Bryan in the White House.

Harper's Weekly, Oct. 6, 1900
Courtesy, Harper & Brothers, New York City

Campaign of 1900

The Republican Party stood on its record as producer of a "full dinner pail" for the workingman. The Democrats reindorsed their platform of 1896, and added to it a blast against the Administration's "Imperialism" and the protection given monopolies by the Republicans. Little of this appeared effective in the apathetic campaign that followed.

After renomination, President McKinley repeated his previous tactics of a campaign from the front porch. At the *right* are seen the President and his invalid wife to whom he was touchingly devoted.

The major chore of Republican campaigning fell to the reluctant candidate for Vice President, Gov. Theodore Roosevelt of New York (*below*), who felt he was being promoted into political oblivion.

Harper's Bazar, Aug. 26, 1899
Courtesy, Harper's Bazaar, New York City

Harper's Weekly, Oct. 27, 1900
Courtesy, Harper & Brothers, New York City

William Jennings Bryan (*above*) talked from the stump with vigorous and bitter invective against Republican corruption.

Harper's Weekly, Sept. 23, 1899
Courtesy, Harper & Brothers, New York City

Campaign of 1900 (Continued)

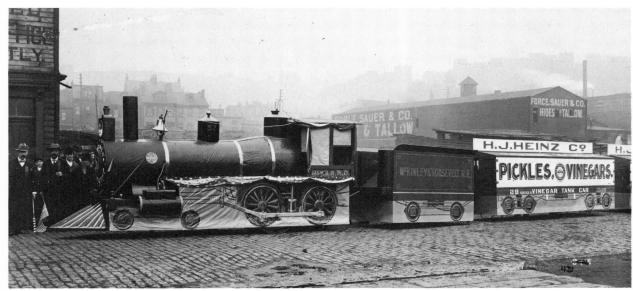

Courtesy, H. J. Heinz Company, Pittsburgh, Pa.

Businessmen rallied behind the Republican ticket and advertised their products along with the candidates, as shown *above*.

Ccl. Roosevelt's war record (see pages 117-119) worked in his favor. At the *right* is a sketch of him in uniform, drawn by Charles Dana Gibson.

Scribner's Magazine, January, 1899

After the polls were closed, the political mathematicians at the two campaign headquarters began to figure the probabilities. *Left.*

Scribner's Magazine June, 1900

5

THE NEW CENTURY

Watch night services of a special solemnity were held in churches all over the nation as the Twentieth Century dawned. There were no signs and portents—although the hectic character of the four years to come might well have been foreshadowed by a few.

President McKinley's victory in November had been an impressive witness to the people's satisfaction with a business government. He received in the vote of the Electoral College 292 tallies as against 155 for William Jennings Bryan, and a popular plurality of over 900,000. He was inaugurated for a second term in March, 1901.

Flanked by Secret Service men, the President went to the Capitol.

"The advance agent of prosperity" delivered his inaugural address against a background of flags.

Both illustrations on this page are from *Harper's Weekly*, Mar. 16, 1901. *Courtesy*, Harper & Brothers, New York City

Northern Pacific Panic

About two months after the inauguration, two of the President's "big business" friends engaged in a struggle for control of the Burlington Railroad that, among other effects, sent the whole list of securities down about thirty points.

Harper's Weekly, Jan. 26, 1901
Courtesy, Harper & Brothers, New York City

J. J. Hill, in Seattle, noticed that the stock of his Northern Pacific Railroad was being bought in larger than normal volume. His banker, J. P. Morgan, was on a holiday in Europe, so Hill came hurrying to Wall Street by special train.

It developed that E. H. Harriman, czar of the Union Pacific, was behind the activity. In reprisal for Hill and Morgan's seizure of control of the Burlington route, Harriman was trying to buy control of the Northern Pacific stock and so get the Burlington by controlling its parent road. From Morgan came an order to buy at any price, in order to hold control.

Above, speculators watching the quotation board.

Right, the rush to buy.

Harper's Weekly, May 18, 1901
Courtesy, Harper & Brothers, New York City

Harper's Weekly, Jan. 26, 1901. Courtesy, Harper & Brothers, New York City

Northern Pacific went to one thousand dollars a share. Frantic selling by traders "caught short" on Northern Pacific sent the whole list down. By noon many stock exchange houses were broke, but Morgan and Harriman allowed the "shorts" to settle and the market steadied.

Left, lights burned all night in the financial district.

Nevada Gold

To add further to the embarrassment of the Democratic Party, new gold strikes were made at Goldfield, Tonopah and Ray, Nev.

The gold hunters headed for the new district by burro pack-train (*right*).

Stagecoaches creaked over narrow canyon trails toward the Gold-field diggings.

The freighting outfit shown *right* operated between Goldfield and Bullfrog, Nev.

All illustrations on this page are by the *courtesy* of the Nevada State Historical Society, Reno

Oil—Texas

Also in the spring of 1901, new wealth spouted out of the earth near Beaumont, Tex. The first well to come in in that section was producing 35,000 barrels a day, and from all over the nation a stampede started to East Texas.

Sleepy little Beaumont forgot all about the lumber and rice business. In jerry-built office buildings like those shown *left* and *below*, thousands of dollars changed hands as company promoters and land-speculators jumped from special trains into action.

At the *left* is shown a section of the tent city which sprang up on Beaumont's vacant lots.

All illustrations on this page are from *Harper's Weekly*, June 22, 1901. *Courtesy*, Harper & Brothers, New York City

Oil—California

Along the coast, south of Santa Barbara, Californian oil production was pushing toward the 1904 high peak of thirty million barrels. In the view *below*, the oil is caught in an improvised storage tank of banked earth.

Harper's Weekly, Mar. 23, 1901. Courtesy, Harper & Brothers, New York City

At Summerland, wells were sunk in the ocean bed, as seen *right*.

Harper's Weekly, Mar. 23, 1901
Courtesy, Harper & Brothers, New York City

The locomotive *below* was specially designed to burn oil. The tremendous demand for gasoline that would come with the low-priced automobile was yet unimagined, and the oil companies were insisting on the superiority of oil to coal as a general fuel.

Harper's Weekly, Oct. 18, 1902
Courtesy, Harper & Brothers, New York City

McKinley Assassinated

Harper's Weekly, June 8, 1901. Courtesy, Harper & Brothers, New York City

The Pan-American Exposition, held at Buffalo, N. Y., was intended to display the progress of the nation through a full century. President McKinley finished his speech at the Temple of Music (*above,* at the left) on Sept. 6, 1901, and stood shaking hands with a long line of visitors. An anarchist, Leon Czolgosz, pushed up in the line and fired two quick shots into the President's body.

Harper's Weekly, Sept. 21, 1901. Courtesy, Harper & Brothers, New York City

Among other watchers at the Millburn house where the President wavered for eight days between life and death were Vice-President Roosevelt and Mark Hanna (*left*).

The wanton stupidity of the act and the general personal regard most Americans had for the President kept anxious groups outside newspaper offices as bulletin followed bulletin. On September 14, Vice-President Roosevelt took the oath of office as President, for McKinley had not survived his wounds.

Harper's Weekly, Sept. 14, 1901. Courtesy, Harper & Brothers, New York City

Why Prophets Are Without Honor

In response to President Theodore Roosevelt's first proclamation, the national press blossomed with editorials. Among others of similar character were:

'The McKinley policy is the Roosevelt policy"—*Washington Post.*

"Discretion and conservatism will be still further developed in President Roosevelt" —*Boston Globe.*

But by the end of 1901, it was evident that inevitable change was at work, and that the President was not its foe.

O. Henry's City

Even sacred Fifth Avenue was conscious of change, for it had been invaded south of 32nd Street by the signs of trade (*right*), and the sidestreet brownstones were declining into rooming houses. So it was when William Sydney Porter discovered New York City in 1902 and mirrored its life in his short stories of the *Four Million.*

Town & Country, Oct. 31, 1903. Courtesy, Town & Country, New York City

Harper's Weekly, Dec. 21, 1901
Courtesy, Harper & Brothers, New York City

The shopping district still centered on 23rd Street near Sixth Avenue (*above*), but "uptown" was beckoning.

The New and the Old

Harper's Weekly, Apr. 25, 1903
Courtesy, Harper & Brothers, New York City

A 1903 specimen of the Automat is shown in the sketch at the *left*. "The whole service of lunch or dinner takes about a minute," observed the caption writer for *Harper's Weekly*.

In 1902, the Escalator pictured *right* was installed at R. H. Macy's New York store. The first Escalator used in this country had been set up in Gimbel's Philadelphia shop after its display at the Paris Exposition of 1900.

Courtesy, Otis Elevator Company, New York City

A patch of green amid the drab walls of East 29th Street and a romantic witness of New York's tolerance was the "Little Church Around the Corner," the Church of the Transfiguration, whose garden is shown *left*.

Town & Country, Aug. 15, 1903
Courtesy, Town & Country, New York City

Pittsburgh

The infant aluminum industry, founded at Pittsburgh in 1888, was now making profits through the growing demand for light-weight automobile bodies.

Right, the new Kensington plant of the Pittsburgh Reduction Company, ca. 1904.

Courtesy, Aluminum Company of America, Pittsburgh, Pa.

Over the city hung a pall of smoke that was the subject of endless jokes. *Below* is seen a view of part of the city from across the Allegheny River, a background to the pageantry with which Heinz's original pickle works was moved from Sharpsburg to Pittsburgh.

Courtesy, H. J. Heinz Company, Pittsburgh, Pa.

57 Varieties

The transformation and packaging of the humble bean—to say nothing of the 56 other products —grew with the growing city.

At the turn of the century, the beans were weighed and wrapped by hand, as shown to the *left* and *below*.

Relishes and ketchups were also hand-labeled and wrapped.

All illustrations on this page are by the *courtesy* of the H. J. Heinz Company, Pittsburgh, Pa.

The Midwest

As the cities of the Midwest grew in population and wealth, their changing manners and racial constituencies were to provide rich material for the novelists of the new century.

Photo by W. H. Bass Co., Indianapolis, Ind.-*Courtesy*, The Indiana Historical Society, Indianapolis

The view of Indianapolis, Ind., *above*, looks northeast from Illinois and Washington streets. The automobile does not dominate the scene.

The rear of the flour milling district of Minneapolis, Minn., is seen in the picture *below*, as it looked around 1901.

Courtesy, Minnesota Historical Society, St. Paul

The Midwest (Continued)

Courtesy, Wisconsin State Historical Society, Madison

Depere, Wis., is seen at the *left* as it appeared at the turn of the century.

The view *right* shows the Milwaukee River, looking southwest from the old Wisconsin Street bridge.

Courtesy, Wisconsin State Historical Society, Madison

Specially constructed ice-breaking ferryboats carried loaded freight cars from port to port along the Great Lakes.

Harper's Weekly, Mar. 1, 1902. Courtesy, Harper & Brothers, New York City

Midwestern Industry

Slowly but surely, the Midwest area was taking over a new industry—the manufacture of automobiles and their accessories. The advertisements reproduced *below* tell the story.

The Cadillac

The Automobile that Solves the Problem

Until the Cadillac was made, all automobile construction was more or less experimental. This machine is made on a new system developed from the experiences of all previous makers: the faults and weaknesses of the old methods have been avoided and a new ideal of motor travel developed that gives a perfect vehicle for comfort, speed, absolute safety, greatest durability, simplicity of operation, wide radius of travel, and reliability under all conditions of roads. You should not buy before examining this wonderful new machine. Price f. o. b. at factory, $750.

The new tonneau attachment, at an extra cost of $100, gives practically two motor vehicles in one, with a seating capacity of two or four, as required—a very graceful effect in either use. Write for illustrated booklet M.

CADILLAC AUTOMOBILE COMPANY, Detroit, Mich.

Harper's Weekly, Mar. 8, 1902
Courtesy, Harper & Brothers, New York City

HAYNES-APPERSON AUTO-MOBILES

Results Count

WIN EVERYTHING

Two Machines entered.
Two Machines receive first certificate.
Two Machines make higher average than any other machines made in America—our record in New York and Buffalo endurance test.
First Prize Long Island endurance test, 100 miles without a stop.
First Prize Cup Five-Mile speed contest, Fort Erie track, Buffalo, N. Y.
First Prize Cup Ten-Mile speed contest, Point Grasse track, Detroit, Mich.

Gold Medal Pan-American Exposition.

Every machine we have ever entered in any contest has won first place. No failure mars our record. We believe this is not true of any other make in the world. Write for catalogue describing our two and four passenger vehicles.

The HAYNES-APPERSON CO.,
Kokomo, Ind., U. S. A.

Harper's Weekly, Feb. 7, 1903
Courtesy, Harper & Brothers, New York City

The best thing on wheels

The Oldsmobile

Physicians use the Oldsmobile in preference to any other because it saves time—and a Doctor's time is money. The Oldsmobile has proved itself by long, hard service to be the ideal Motor Vehicle for Physicians. It outwears a dozen horses, is always harnessed, always fed—is built to run and does it. All months are good months for the Oldsmobile, but the autumn months are best of all. If you want prompt delivery, order promptly.

Price $650.00 f. o. b. Detroit

Write for book 21, which tells all about it.

SELLING AGENTS

Oldsmobile Co., 138 W. 38th St., New York
Oldsmobile Co., 1124 Connecticut Ave., Washington, D. C.
Quaker City Auto. Co., 128 No. Broad St., Philadelphia
H. B. Shattuck & Son, 239 Columbus Ave., Boston
Banker Bros. Co., East End, Pittsburgh
Oldsmobile Co., 411 Euclid Ave., Cleveland, Ohio
William E. Metzger, 254 Jefferson Ave., Detroit
Ralph Temple & Austrian Co., 293 Wabash Ave., Chicago
Fisher Automobile Co., Indianapolis
Olds Gasoline Engine Works, Omaha
W. C. Jaynes Auto. Co., 873 Main St., Buffalo, N. Y.
Day Automobile Co., St. Louis and Kansas City, Mo.
George Hannan, 1455 California St., Denver
Clark & Hawkins, 903 Texas Ave., Houston, Tex.
The Manufacturers Co., 26 Fremont St., San Francisco
A. F. Chase & Co., 215 So. Third St., Minneapolis
Oldsmobile Co., 708 National Ave., Milwaukee, Wis.
Abbott Cycle Co., 411 Baronne St., New Orleans, La.
Autovehicle Co., 79 Orange St., Newark, N. J.
Hyslop Bros., Toronto, Canada
Rochester Automobile Co., 170 South Ave., Rochester, N. Y.
Mason's Carriage Works, Davenport, Ia.
C. H. Johnson, 55 So. Forsyth St., Atlanta, Ga.
Sutcliffe & Co., 411 Main St., Louisville, Ky.
Texas Implement and Machine Co., Dallas, Tex.
Jas. B. Seager, Tuscan, Ariz.

Olds Motor Works
Detroit, Mich., U. S. A.

DETACHABLE DOUBLE TUBE TIRE

The superiority of Diamond Single Tube tires will be found in our Double Tube Detachable

DIAMOND TIRES

Write for valuable opinions of users

THE DIAMOND RUBBER CO.

AKRON, OHIO.

New York-170 Broadway
Boston-234 Congress St.
Buffalo-41 Court Street
Philadelphia-435 N. Broad St.
Detroit-310 Woodward Ave.
Chicago-420 Wabash Ave.
Denver-1655 Blake St.
San Francisco-8 Beale St.
Cleveland-41 Euclid Ave.

SINGLE TUBE

Harper's Weekly, Feb. 7, 1903
Courtesy, Harper & Brothers, New York City

Harper's Weekly, Aug. 23, 1902. Courtesy, Harper & Brothers, New York City

Mass Production

By concentrating all his equipment and skill on the manufacture of one model in large volume, R. E. Olds brought the automobile within reach of ordinary citizens.

The 1901 Oldsmobile shown at the *left* was one of the famous "curved-dash" runabouts. More than four hundred were sold in the first year of production (see advertisement on page 167).

The state of the nation's roads in 1901 made the rather primitive testing method seen at the *right* a valid guide to "actual operation" of the Oldsmobile.

In 1903 an Oldsmobile was produced specially equipped to run on rails.

The "New" South

Although, by 1901, Southern manufacturing and industry were conforming perforce to the Northern pattern, the psychology of Southern people remained different, and few of their ancient social problems seemed on the way to solution.

The new textile mills in Georgia were controlled largely by Northern capital. The mill shown *right* was at Augusta.

Harper's Weekly, Oct. 10, 1903
Courtesy, Harper & Brothers, New York City

Harper's Weekly, Oct. 10, 1903. Courtesy, Harper & Brothers, New York City

The wharves at Savannah, Ga., cleared immense quantities of naval stores at the expense of Georgia's and Carolina's forests.

In the Kentucky mountains a forgotten population went quietly against all modern trends. A "moonshine" still is shown in the sketch to the *right*.

Scribner's Magazine, April, 1901

The "Old" South

Each year the Confederate Memorial Day brought out the old flags and aroused again the old feelings. The picture *below* was taken in Richmond, Va., early in the new century.

Courtesy, The Valentine Museum, Richmond, Va.

The Southern Negro cherished the thought of a "better day coming." The baptismal ceremony shown *left* took place in Wake County, N. C., around 1903.

Little or nothing had been done to provide a workable way of life for Negroes to replace the paternalism bred of slavery.

Courtesy, North Carolina State Department of Archives and History, Raleigh

Country Roads

The earlier automobiles had "shown up" the condition of the nation's roads, and now with the low-priced car in view a real effort was made to improve secondary roads as well as highways.

An appeal was made to local pride for the furtherance of the "Good Roads" program. At the *right*, a crusher is seen at work.

Harper's Weekly, Apr. 5, 1902. Courtesy, Harper & Brothers, New York City

Courtesy, Public Roads Administration, Washington, D. C.

Less elaborate was the horse-drawn "drag" shown to the *left*.

The R.F.D. driver no longer had the old excuse that he "got stuck in the mud" when he operated over a road like the one shown *right*, near Jackson, Tenn.

Courtesy, Public Roads Administration, Washington, D. C.

Oklahoma Opening

When the former Kiowa-Comanche lands were declared open in 1901, the homesteaders were obliged to register and the tracts were assigned by a lottery. This was done in an effort to prevent the usual, disorderly homestead "run."

Harper's Weekly, Aug. 10, 1901. *Courtesy*, Harper & Brothers, New York City

At Lawton, near Fort Sill, prospective homesteaders waited in tents for the day of the drawing. *Above.*

Harper's Weekly, Aug. 10, 1901. *Courtesy*, Harper & Brothers, New York City

It was estimated that eighteen thousand land-hungry persons camped in El Reno (*left*), another point where registration was made.

Twelve days after the opening, Hobart, Okla., county seat of Kiowa County, had built up to the proportions shown in the view *right.*

Courtesy, Scribner Art File

Water in the Deserts

1901 was a drought year, and this circumstance heightened popular interest in the Congressional debates over the Reclamation Act, Federal irrigation projects and a tighter policy on public land administration.

An electrically pumped artesian well fed the Arizona irrigation system shown *right*.

Harper's Weekly, June 21, 1902. Courtesy, Harper & Brothers, New York City

The orchard near Phoenix, Ariz., at the *left*, grew in soil formerly considered barren.

Harper's Weekly, Aug. 30, 1902. Courtesy, Harper & Brothers, New York City

A Montana distribution flume is seen at the *right*.

Scribner's Magazine, June, 1902

Water in the Deserts (Continued)

Over the hills came a redwood-stave pipe line with water for the orange groves near Corona, Calif.

Illustrated World, Technical World, Vol. I, 1904
Courtesy, Popular Mechanics, Chicago, Ill.

Pumping plants like the one at the *right* fed water to the newly established rice-growing industry of southwestern Louisiana.

Harper's Weekly, Apr. 19, 1902. *Courtesy*, Harper & Brothers, New York City

New towns sprang up to handle the mounting shipments of rice from Louisiana land that had once been useless prairie.

Harper's Weekly, Apr. 19, 1902
Courtesy, Harper & Brothers, New York City

Society Amuses Itself

A new game was imported from England in the winter of 1901.

"Ping Pong has taken vigorous hold of Society. Most dinner parties this spring end in an informal tournament."

Harper's Weekly, May 10, 1902
Courtesy, Harper & Brothers, New York City

Courtesy, Mr. Myron F. Henkel, Springfield, Ill.

Balmy days brought out the golfers in Springfield, Ill. (*left*).

But at Hot Springs, N. C., the golfing enthusiasts could play all through the winter as seen in the picture to the *right*.

Town & Country, Jan. 17, 1903
Courtesy, Town & Country, New York City

Less Strenuous Amusements

Town & Country, Aug. 20, 1904. *Courtesy*, Town & Country, New York City

For the artistic young lady, certain carefully supervised art classes provided a polite Bohemian atmosphere and the rudiments of drawing.

Sitting and watching others amuse themselves has always had its devotees. In the picture at the *right* is shown a section of the grandstand at the Point Judith Country Club Horse Show, Narragansett, R. I.

Town & Country, Sept. 3, 1904
Courtesy, Town & Country, New York City

Courtesy, Mr. Myron F. Henkel, Springfield, Ill.

Sitting on a front porch of noble size and gracious appointments, like the one seen at the *left*, was a soothing experience on a summer day—before the invention of the radio.

Auto Racing

Owners of elaborate motor cars liked to try the endurance of their "machines."

At the *right*, the entry of White Steamers are lined up for the start of the New York to Boston endurance "run" of 1902.

Courtesy, Scribner Art File

Courtesy, Pomona Public Library, Calif.

The first annual "run" of the Auto Club of Southern California in 1904 ended in a big dinner at the Hotel Polomares, Pomona, Calif. At the *left* are shown the survivors of the trip, ready for the feast.

Manufacturers were interested in the prestige that came from record smashing and encouraged professional drivers like Barney Oldfield. He is the driver of the Cooper car pictured *right* at Empire City track in 1903.

Town & Country, June 13, 1903. *Courtesy*, Town & Country, New York City

Frippery in the New Century

Chief among the fashionable fads in dress for 1900 and a few years thereafter was the shirt-waist vogue.

The shirtwaist style shown *left* was made with a plain French back and was considered very "effective and timely" for 1901. The group of ladies shown *below* were residents of the new mining town of Goldfield, Nev. (see page 157), but as this picture proves, they were very much *à la mode de New York*.

Harper's Bazar, January, 1901
Courtesy, Harper's Bazaar, New York City

Courtesy, Nevada State Historical Society, Reno

Left is a gown worn by Mrs. Theodore Roosevelt in 1902.

To the *right* is seen a new hat for 1903, "a large, black, picture-hat with the new, high crown and cut-steel buckles."

Courtesy, Smithsonian Institution, Washington, D. C.

Harper's Bazar, October, 1903
Courtesy, Harper's Bazaar, New York City

Lingerie, etc.

The petticoat to the *right* was made of turquoise taffeta and trimmed with Valenciennes lace.

At the *left* is shown a pair of embroidered silk hose, style of 1902.

Harper's Bazar, March, 1901
Courtesy, Harper's Bazaar, New York City

Town & Country, Oct. 25, 1902
Courtesy, Town & Country, New York City

The object on the *right* was a black satin chest-protector "to be worn with evening dress."

Harper s Bazar, June, 1901
Courtesy, Harper's Bazaar, New York City

Harper's Weekly, Apr. 25, 1903
Courtesy, Harper & Brothers, New York City

The Home Journal, Jan. 17, 1901
Courtesy, Town & Country, New York City

Above. "A thorough protection against dust and sunburn."

In describing the suit shown *above*, the fashion writer let herself go as follows: "A daring design in blue broadcloth! The bolero is *assertive*!"

Horse Play

A meet of the Meadowbrook hounds at Jericho, Long Island, N. Y., is seen *above*. In 1904, when this picture was taken, fox-hunting was becoming more popular than following the drag.

The picture *below* shows an incident in the polo match between Princeton and Squadron "A" at Van Cortlandt Park, N. Y., on May 14, 1904.

Both illustrations on this page are from *Harper's Weekly*, June 4, 1904. *Courtesy*, Harper & Brothers, New York City

The Seventy-Five Million

The census of 1900 set the population of the United States at just under seventy-six million. Of these, the overwhelming majority lived outside the pleasant, rarefied atmosphere of the preceding five pages.

Immigrants poured through the new receiving station on Ellis Island in New York harbor, to find that what loose gold had been lying about the streets had already been garnered.

Harper's Weekly, Jan. 19, 1901. *Courtesy*, Harper & Brothers, New York City

Harper's Weekly, May 18, 1901. *Courtesy*, Harper & Brothers, New York City

But the cosmopolitan city received them hospitably, and their children took up America's ways. The May Pole celebration in Battery Park shown at the *left* took place in 1901.

On the western prairies the farmer came to town and found street fairs in progress, ready to catch his eye and his money.

Harper's Weekly, Aug. 31, 1901
Courtesy, Harper & Brothers, New York City

The Seventy-Five Million (Continued)

Opportunity awaited everyone. The optimism of the years of the full dinner-pail was contagious.

Courtesy, Mack-International Motor Truck Corporation, New York City

It was said that science would create new jobs faster than technological improvements could throw men out of work. Skilled mechanics like the Mack Truck builders shown *left* need never worry.

The Steel Works Club "smoker" seen at the *right* was hailed as a great step toward better labor-management relations.

Illustrated World, Technical World, Vol. I, 1904
Courtesy, Popular Mechanics, Chicago, Ill.

At political barbecues, the faithful followers of the local boss gathered to praise his name and eat the roast meat of municipal corruption.

Harper's Weekly, Sept. 13, 1902. *Courtesy*, Harper & Brothers, New York City

Family

In the plain folk's world, at the start of the new century, the family was paramount. Men worked for their families; their common aim was to "leave the family comfortable."

Courtesy. Mrs. Frank Ewing, Grand Rapids, Mich.

Members of families enjoyed one another's company, as a rule. Picnics like the one shown *above* were family affairs.

A very typical family man of around 1903 was Alfred E. Smith (at the *left* with Mrs. Smith).

From The Alfred E. Smith Collection
Courtesy. Museum of the City of New York

The grim story of Carry Nation (*right*) and her saloon-smashing crusade started with a family broken by drink.

Courtesy. Scribner Art File

Sport from the Stands

College football was growing into a spectacle. At the Harvard-Yale game on Nov. 23, 1901 (shown *below*), thirty-six thousand people were on hand to see Harvard win by 22 to 0.

Harper's Weekly, Dec. 7, 1901. *Courtesy,* Harper & Brothers, New York City

Professional baseball attracted larger and larger crowds to watch the city teams battle for League pennants, and, after 1903, in the "World Series." The picture *below* was taken at a game between New York and Chicago (National League) as "better than forty thousand people crowded the New York Polo Grounds."

Harper's Weekly, July 2, 1904. *Courtesy,* Harper & Brothers, New York City

Basketball

The one popular sport which is completely American in origin had grown greatly in popularity since its invention by James Naismith in 1891. It had become a recognized intercollegiate sport, and was played by girls and boys of all ages.

Junior basketeers from a Chicago suburb are seen at the *right*, in the traditional grouping around their coach.

Courtesy, Ravenswood-Lake View Historical Association, sponsored by The Chicago Public Library, Ill.

Harper's Weekly, Feb. 22, 1902. Courtesy, Harper & Brothers, New York City

A girls' team from a Brookline, Mass., school is shown in action at the *left*.

"Do or die" must have been the motto of this University of Nebraska Varsity Team.

Courtesy, Public Relations Office, University of Nebraska, Lincoln

Theater

New stars, shoddy plays and managers' feuds characterized the American stage at the start of the new century.

Town & Country, May 16, 1903. Courtesy, Town & Country, New York City

David Warfield in *The Auctioneer* (*left*) scored a 1903 triumph.

Miss Maxine Elliott (*below*) was displaying her brunette beauty in Clyde Fitch's *Her Own Way.*

Town & Country, Oct. 18, 1902
Courtesy, Town & Country, New York City

Miss Ethel Barrymore in a 1902 sketch entitled *Carrots* was said to have "a deft and gracious art which conceals art."

Town & Country, Oct. 3, 1903
Courtesy, Town & Country, New York City

Film and Frou-Frou

Spurred on by declining public interest in the "movies," an Edison cameraman shot a film in 1903 based on an original, plotted story and produced the first American drama in motion pictures: *The Great Train Robbery*. A still from this epic of the screen is shown *below*, complete with flicker effect.

Courtesy, Film Library, The Museum of Modern Art, New York City

Town & Country, Oct. 10, 1903. Courtesy, Town & Country, New York City

A scene from a 1903 musical comedy is shown *above* to prove that, like the Rock of Gibraltar, musical comedy never changes in essentials.

Hits of 1904

Courtesy, Robinson Locke Collection, The New York Public Library, New York City

The year 1904 found George M. Cohan singing "Give My Regards to Broadway" in *Little Johnny Jones* (left). He wrote the play, staged it, composed the music and took the star part.

Earlier that year, Arnold Daly had produced a "pleasant play" by George Bernard Shaw entitled *Candida*. A scene from the 1904 New York production is shown at the *right*.

A Souvenir of Candida. Courtesy, The New York Public Library, New York City

Courtesy, Purdue University, Lafayette, Ind.

At the *left* is a scene from the 1904 production of George Ade's *College Widow*—the first stage treatment of American undergraduate life, and, naturally enough, a comedy.

At Home

A desire to identify themselves with the older cultures of Europe had long since influenced the opulent in their choice of house decoration. This fashion was now beginning to influence the "comfortably well off."

Decorators seemed particularly fond of reproducing the elegant pomp of the French Courts for their customers in Pennsylvania and New York (to the *right* and *below*).

Harper's Weekly, Dec. 1, 1900. *Courtesy,* Harper & Brothers, New York City

The Home Journal, Jan. 24, 1901. *Courtesy,* Town & Country, New York City

But Mrs. Theodore Roosevelt, the new mistress of the White House, planned the colonial garden shown at the *right*.

Harper's Bazar, November, 1904. *Courtesy,* Harper's Bazaar, New York City

Simpler Style

The older Victorian virtues continued to be expressed in the homes of public men.

In the Governor's Mansion at Lincoln, Neb. (shown *left* and *below*), any decorative innovations would have caused too much caustic comment.

Courtesy, Nebraska State Historical Society, Lincoln

Courtesy, Nebraska State Historical Society, Lincoln

Nor could the Judge, a corner of whose living room is seen at the *left,* afford implied rebukes to popular taste.

Courtesy, Nevada State Historical Society, Reno

Oddments in Decoration

A "cosy corner" is at the left of the room shown *right*. Note the decorative iron stove, the wicker rocking chair and the portieres.

Typical room of a girl at the University of Nebraska in 1902 is shown *left*.

A Lincoln, Neb., dentist provided this waiting room for his clients at the start of the new century. No symbols of his craft are visible except the pile of magazines on the table.

All illustrations on this page are by the *courtesy* of the Nebraska State Historical Society, Lincoln

Kitchens

The reform movement in interior decoration extended to the housewife's workshop. Mounting numbers of city people who lived in "flats" or apartments found the kitchen very close under their eyes and noses. Furthermore, "the absence of a maid's sitting-room in apartments makes it an ethical obligation upon the employer to provide a commodious and practical kitchen," said the editor of *Harper's Bazar*.

The tiled chimney effect in the kitchen at the *left* was considered an innovation in 1901.

Harper's Bazar, January, 1901
Courtesy, Harper's Bazaar, New York City

The use of white paint in the kitchen at the *right* was supposed to set off the sheen of the copper pots and pans.

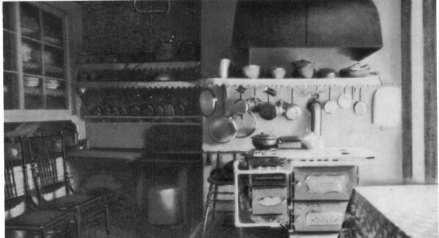

Harper's Bazar, January, 1901. *Courtesy*, Harper's Bazaar, New York City

In April, 1901, a daring designer projected the "all-electric" kitchen sketched at the *left*.

Harper's Bazar, April, 1901. *Courtesy*, Harper's Bazaar, New York City

Barrooms

Possibly at the request of their customers, saloon-keepers permitted their establishments to be photographed only at slack hours of trade.

The four-sided bar at the old Waldorf-Astoria, New York City, is seen at the *right*.

Local industry was featured in the mineral display case at the right of the Tonopah, Nev., bar shown *below*.

Courtesy, The Waldorf-Astoria, New York City

Courtesy, Nevada State Historical Society, Reno

6
SHADOW OF THE BIG STICK

Physical and social changes in the United States already pictured in Chapter 5 were paralleled by upheavals in politics and industry. "Speak softly," Theodore Roosevelt had said early in his career, "and carry a big stick." By December, 1901, the nation found that the big stick could be swung as well as carried; that the President was a reformer at heart.

W. H. Hillyer, *James Talcott: Merchant.* 1937

First domestic victim was J. P. Morgan's railroad trust, the National Securities Corporation. Government prosecution under the Sherman Act was begun against it in February, 1902.

Conservative businessmen like the New York merchant shown *above* wondered what the world was coming to.

In the picture of Wall Street at the *right,* the flags were at half-mast for President McKinley's death. The scene expresses equally well the "Street's" reaction to the "treason" of a Republican President against finance.

Harper's Weekly, Sept. 21, 1901
Courtesy, Harper & Brothers, New York City

Harper's Weekly, May 30, 1903
Courtesy, Harper & Brothers, New York City

The view at the *left* shows the President, the Governor of Arizona, the head of the Santa Fe Railroad and the President of Columbia University standing at the Grand Canyon.

Tours around the country in such oddly-assorted company were part of the President's strategy to enlist popular support for his policies.

Anthracite Strike

On May 12, 1902, the entire body of anthracite coal miners went on strike for adjustment of wages and hours of work, but primarily to secure recognition of their union by the mine operators.

There was little violence, but the miners were determined to stick it out. All through the summer and autumn of 1902 no coal was dug at the Branchdale Colliery near Minersville, Pa. (*right*), or at any other anthracite works.

Harper's Weekly, Nov. 1, 1902. Courtesy, Harper & Brothers, New York City

As the price of coal rose from five dollars a ton to almost thirty, the gathering up of lumps that fell from barges (as seen in the sketch *left*) became a profitable minor business. Schools were closed; industries shut down and a winter of tragedy was in prospect.

Harper's Weekly, Oct. 18, 1902. Courtesy, Harper & Brothers, New York City

The President exhausted all diplomatic means of settlement. He had made up his mind to protect the public interest by seizure and military operation of the mines, when, at the October 14 conference sketched *right*, Elihu Root, J. P. Morgan and the President worked out a plan for an arbitration commission which settled the strike. It was a great personal triumph for Theodore Roosevelt.

Harper's Weekly, Oct. 25, 1902. Courtesy, Harper & Brothers, New York City

Army and Navy

Meanwhile all encouragement was given the armed services by the President. A man who had been Assistant Secretary of the Navy and was author of a history of the Navy's part in the War of 1812 was not a President to let barnacles cluster on the warships or their personnel.

In June, 1902, he attended the Centennial Exercises at West Point (left).

Harper's Weekly, June 21, 1902
Courtesy, Harper & Brothers, New York City

August, 1903, he reviewed the Fleet from the bridge of the Presidential yacht *Mayflower*.

Harper's Weekly, Aug. 29, 1903
Courtesy, Harper & Brothers, New York City

But more significant than pageantry, the launching of the new armored warship *Pennsylvania* at Cramp's shipyard, Philadelphia (left), and the promise of many more such vessels to come, served notice on the world of 1903 that the "big stick" could reach across water.

Harper's Weekly, Sept. 12, 1903. *Courtesy*, Harper & Brothers, New York City

Submarines

Experiments with undersea boats were continued, along with development of new types of surface craft and improvements in armor and ordnance.

In 1902 the Navy Department tried out the *Adder* (right) in Peconic Bay, Long Island, N. Y.

Harper's Weekly, Nov. 29, 1902
Courtesy, Harper & Brothers, New York City

Simon Lake's boat *Protector* (shown *left* in sectional view) was tested under the eye of Navy experts. *Below*, the *Protector* is shown in cruising trim.

Illustrated World, Technical World, Vol. I, 1904
Courtesy, Popular Mechanics, Chicago, Ill.

Illustrated World, Technical World, Vol. I, 1904
Courtesy, Popular Mechanics, Chicago, Ill.

Where Men Were Men

President Roosevelt was pleased when the public associated him with the young and still expanding West rather than with his native New York.

Courtesy, The Library of the University of Texas, Austin

He could have held his own in the hurly-burly of the Kimble County, Tex., land rush seen at the *left*.

The snows of a Nevada winter would have been a challenge to his hardihood. The picture shown *right* was taken in Virginia City.

Courtesy, Nevada State Historical Society, Reno

The railroad surveying party shown *left* at Cleburne, Tex., would have found in him a hearty trail companion.

Courtesy, The Library of the University of Texas, Austin

Mushrooming Towns

The West had vigor and life. Its towns were hopeful and democratic.

Courtesy, Nevada State Historical Society, Reno

Goldfield, Nev., *above*, was the center of a mining boom (see page 157).

The north side of El Campo, Tex., *below*, was in 1903 still typical of the frontier.

Courtesy, The Library of the University of Texas, Austin

Conservation

The West was more than a romantic backdrop for the strenuous life. It was a region where heedless and wasteful industries had done damage to national resources. Some kind of regulation seemed imperative.

The new oil industry did little or nothing to prevent calamities like that shown *left*.

Harper's Weekly, Oct. 24, 1903
Courtesy, Harper & Brothers, New York City

It remained to be seen whether the cattle industry had been a blessing or a curse to the West.

Photograph by W. H. Jackson. *Courtesy*, The Edison Institute, Dearborn, Mich.

In the northern Mid-West, the lumbermen continued their waste among the forests.

Courtesy, Minnesota Historical Society, St. Paul

Water, Water Everywhere

The spring of 1903 brought disastrous floods to the West and South, and intensified the drive for flood-control.

In Topeka, Kans., the rampaging river flooded Kansas Avenue, *right*, and a pontoon bridge was hastily thrown across that thoroughfare.

Harper's Weekly, June 13, 1903. Courtesy, Harper & Brothers, New York City

Union Station at Kansas City, *left*, knew an unwonted quiet as three feet of water flooded up to the ticket windows.

At Clifton, S. C., flood waters wrecked the mill in the background (*below*) and washed out the trolley tracks.

Harper's Weekly, June 20, 1903
Courtesy, Harper & Brothers, New York City

Harper's Weekly, June 27, 1903. Courtesy, Harper & Brothers, New York City

Up in the Air

Man had dreamed for centuries of controlled flight through the air. The capricious balloon was not enough of a triumph over nature's laws.

As early as 1900, Orville and Wilbur Wright, bicycle builders of Dayton, Ohio, had tested a glider like the one shown *left* at Kitty Hawk, N. C. In October, 1902, several glides of over 600 feet were made.

Courtesy, Scribner Art File

Prof. S. P. Langley had been experimenting since 1896 with a motor-driven air-ship. On Oct. 7, 1903, the Langley machine, shown *right* on its launching catapult, fell into the Potomac at Widewater, Va., "like a handful of mortar." At another test in December it failed again.

Harper's Weekly, Sept. 19, 1903. Courtesy, Harper & Brothers, New York City

The Wright brothers knew from their glider trials the exact amount of power necessary to sustain their ship in flight. They built a suitable engine and propellors. Then on Dec. 17, 1903, at Kitty Hawk, Orville Wright piloted the first flight ever made by a heavier-than-air machine. At the *left* is shown the original Wright plane in flight.

Courtesy, North Carolina State Department of Archives and History, Raleigh

Ford

Henry Ford and eleven other stockholders formed the Ford Motor Company in June, 1903, so beginning a new phase in automobile history.

The low-priced Model "A" shown *right* appeared in 1903.

Courtesy, Detroit Public Library, Mich.

The FORD MOTOR CAR

In the eyes of the Chauffeur

is the most satisfactory Automobile made for every-day service. The two cylinder (opposed) motor gives 8 actual horsepower, and eliminates the vibration so noticeable in other machines. The body is luxurious and comfortable and can be removed from the chassis by loosening six bolts.

Price with Tonneau, $900.00
As a Runabout, $800.00
Standard equipment includes 3-inch heavy double tube tires

We agree to assume all responsibility in any action the TRUST may take regarding alleged infringement of the Selden Patent to prevent you from buying the Ford—"*The Car of Satisfaction.*"

We Hold the World's Record

The Ford "999" (the fastest machine in the world), driven by Mr. Ford, made a mile in 39½ seconds—equal to 92 miles an hour.
Write for illustrated catalogue and name of our nearest agent.

Ford Motor Co., Detroit, Mich.

Harper's Weekly, Feb. 13, 1904
Courtesy, Harper & Brothers, New York City

National advertising like the specimen at the *left* put Ford in active competition for control of the cheap car field:

Note the statement: "We agree to assume all responsibility in any action the TRUST may take regarding alleged infringement of the SELDEN PATENT." The holders of this patent claimed royalties on all cars driven by internal combustion engines—a claim not finally disallowed until 1911.

The Mack Avenue plant shown *right* was the 1903 version of River Rouge.

Courtesy, Detroit Public Library, Mich.

Telephone

The invention of the loading coil in 1900 by Michael Pupin greatly increased the efficiency of long-distance transmission. In the picture at the *left*, three loading coils are seen mounted on the pole.

Below is shown a clever 1903 adaptation of the automobile, designed in Raleigh, N. C., especially to haul telephone poles.

Courtesy, Western Electric Company, New York City

The dial telephone, or automatic system, was found in an increasing number of places. A dial phone of 1904 is shown directly *below*.

Courtesy, North Carolina State Department of Archives and History, Raleigh

Illustrated World, Technical World, Vol. II, 1904-05.

Courtesy, Popular Mechanics, Chicago, Ill.

Above is a view of the automatic telephone exchange at Lincoln, Neb., late in 1904.

Dots and Dashes

In 1902 Marconi set up a send-receive station at Glace Bay, Nova Scotia, and achieved the first West-to-East radio transmission across the Atlantic.

The interior of the Glace Bay station is seen at the *right*, and the antenna system is shown *below*.

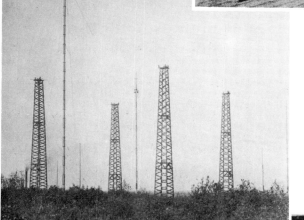

The value of radio (or wireless if one prefers) as a safety device on shipboard was immediately apparent. The *S. S. Minnehaha* in 1904 used the installation shown *below*.

All illustrations on this page are by the *courtesy* of the Radio Corporation of America, New York City

Steam and Steel

Although the principle of the steam turbine was simple, problems of design and construction had held up its general employment in power plants. But by 1901 American engineers felt they had their problems solved in a new and radically different type of machine.

A power station on Fiske Street, Chicago, contracted to use a 5000 kilowatt turbine of the new type and stipulated delivery in the spring of 1903.

The picture at the *left* shows the first commercial Curtis-Emmet turbine-generator combination as it made the deadline at Chicago. It took one-tenth the space and weighed one-eighth as much as the reciprocating engines it replaced.

Courtesy, General Electric Company, Schenectady, N. Y.

By 1904, all-steel thrashing machines were on the market as shown *below.*

Courtesy, J. I. Case Company, Racine, Wis.

Brand Names and Symbols

Advertisers were quick to discover the value of associating a product with an easily-remembered name or symbol.

"Bear in mind" was *Pettijohn's* motto; *Force* trusted to Sunny Jim.

Bon Ami's chick "hadn't scratched yet."

"*Ingersoll*" became a slang name for all watches, and any housewife would approve of *Baker's* neat serving-maid.

Baltimore Fire

On Feb. 7, 1904, began the third largest conflagration in the history of American cities. One hundred and fifty acres were burned over in the heart of the business district.

The picture *above* is a view of the city, northeast from Baltimore and Liberty streets, made about 1900. Many of the buildings in this area were destroyed.

In the panorama *below* are seen the ruins along

Both illustrations on this page are by the *courtesy* of The Municipal Museum of the City of Baltimore, Md.

Baltimore Fire (Continued)

Engine companies came on flat-cars from as far away as New York City to aid in stemming the fire.

Above is a view of part of the conflagration at its height.

Baltimore Street, west of St. Paul Street.

Both illustrations on this page are by the *courtesy* of The Municipal Museum of the City of Baltimore, Md.

Meat Strike

Handlers, packers and butchers in the Chicago stock yards went on strike July 12, 1904, charging that the packing-house owners were discriminating against union members. The strike spread to Kansas City, Omaha and other centers.

Courtesy, Scribner Art File

This was the beginning of a series of troubles for the meat-packers which climaxed in 1906 with the publication of *The Jungle*, with a Federal investigation of conditions, and a much stricter government check on what was packed and how it was packed.

A view of the stock yards is shown at the *left. Below,* police hold a crowd of strikers in check at Ashland and 43rd streets, Chicago.

Harper's Weekly, Aug. 27, 1904. *Courtesy,* Harper & Brothers, New York City

Science and Food

The American public was relying more and more for food and medicines on the impersonal, mass-producing, centralized plants which had shouldered aside local food-processers and drug dispensers. Around 1904, it became clear that false claims were being made for many of these products, and that adulteration was a common practice.

Some producers of packaged foods had already set up their own bacteriological laboratories, as shown *right*, and maintained high standards.

Courtesy, H. J. Heinz Company, Pittsburgh, Pa.

Courtesy, Scribner Art File

Dr. Harvey W. Wiley (*left*), chief chemist of the Department of Agriculture, conducted campaigns of public education and made dramatic exposures of offending companies, all of which crystalized popular sentiment in favor of a Federal Pure Food and Drug Act.

At Tuskegee, Ala., Dr. George W. Carver was beginning experiments which led to the discovery of new uses for the sweet potato, soy bean and peanut.

Courtesy, Tuskegee Institute, Alabama

New York Subway

The first unit of the Subway system opened in 1904 and was operated by the Interborough Rapid Transit Company.

The picture at the *left* gives an idea of the difficulties in the way of construction. For a good many years New York's streets were torn up like this periodically, as extensions of the Subway were made.

At the *right* is seen the official party ready for the first Subway ride. The electric power had not been turned on and the inspection car was pushed by one of the old "Elevated" locomotives.

Courtesy, Board of Transporation of The City of New York

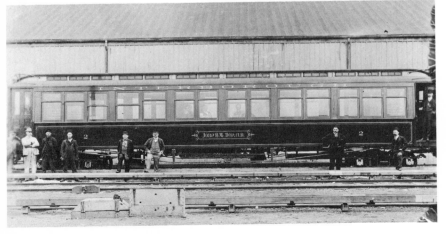

One of the first real Subway cars, delivered and ready for the opening of the system, is shown at the *left*. It bore the name of the contractor who had built the first section of the line.

Courtesy, Board of Transporation of The City of New York

"Meet Me in St. Louis, Louis . . ."

From late April to December, 1904, the city of St. Louis, Mo., celebrated the centennial of the Louisiana Purchase with a great Exposition. It was attended by almost twenty million visitors.

Courtesy, Missouri Historical Society, St. Louis

The Festival Hall and the Cascades are shown *above.*

But "The Pike," a mile of concessions akin to the "Midway" at the Chicago Exposition, was one of the more popular features. It is seen at the *right.*

When the lights went out on the colossal show and the cash deficit was reckoned up, newspaper editors said "it would be in all probability the last big World's Fair."

Harper's Weekly, May 21, 1904
Courtesy, Harper & Brothers, New York City

Campaign of 1904

Mark Hanna's death in February, 1904, left the anti-Roosevelt Republicans without a voice or a rallying-point. They acquiesced sullenly in his unanimous nomination by the Convention at Chicago on June 23.

Harper's Weekly, July 2, 1904. *Courtesy,* Harper & Brothers, New York City

The Republican Convention is shown in session at the *left.*

Formal notification was given the Democratic nominee, Judge Alton B. Parker (extreme right in the picture to the *right*), in an August meeting at Esopus, N. Y.

Harper's Weekly, Aug. 20, 1904. *Courtesy,* Harper & Brothers, New York City

Judge Parker had been opposed as a reactionary by Bryan and a strong minority of the Democrats. Although the financial interests preferred Parker personally to the Republican nominee, they feared the Democratic policies he would be forced to support. The bogey of Bryanism lurked behind Parker. President Roosevelt campaigned strenuously and effectively. In the picture at the *left,* fireworks are being released in New York's Madison Square, as a Republican mass-meeting opened on October 19.

Harper's Weekly, Nov. 5, 1904
Courtesy, Harper & Brothers, New York City

7
STRENUOUS LIVING

Theodore Roosevelt was elected President by a landslide vote—a popular plurality of over two and a half million! Among other trophies, he could boast of wresting Missouri out of the Solid South and into the Republican column. "I am no longer a political accident," he told Mrs. Roosevelt.

Courtesy, Mr. Stephen L. Newnham, Philadelphia, Pa.

As might have been expected, this inaugural parade was a little different. In the view *above* a band of Indians (including Geronimo) is shown passing the Riggs Bank.

At the *left*, an artist's sketch of the President delivering (strenuously) his inaugural address.

Harper's Weekly, Mar. 4, 1905.

Steel

In March, 1901, ten great corporations had combined under the sponsorship of J. P. Morgan to form the United States Steel Corporation. On Jan. 28, 1905, Congress opened the "trust-busting" season with an investigation of practices in the steel industry. The President's war against monopolies had been handsomely endorsed at the polls, but many Americans found a romantic fascination in the very ruthlessness and strength of steel and its manufacture.

Above is shown an old-type charging machine used on an open-hearth furnace at Homestead.

At the *right* yawns the open mouth of a fifteen-ton Bessemer Converter.

The one hundred and forty inch steam driven plate-mill shown at the *left* was installed in 1903 at the Homestead works.

All illustrations on this page are by the *courtesy* of the United States Steel Corporation, New York City

Countryside

Far from the roaring, smoking mills, rural America was undisturbed by the furore in Washington.

The Morgan County, Mo., farmer seen at the *right* went the placid way of his fathers.

Courtesy, Charles van Ravenswaay Collection, Missouri Historical Society, St. Louis

Courtesy, North Carolina State Department of Archives and History, Raleigh

Wild ponies were corralled on the beach near Beaufort, N. C.

The picture from Camden County, Mo., at the *right* shows how rafts of ties were floated downstream to market.

Courtesy, Charles van Ravenswaay Collection, Missouri Historical Society, St. Louis

Country Folk

From the Jacob A. Riis Collection. *Courtesy,* Museum of the City of New York

Life was comfortable for the corner-store lounger shown *above*, so long as Maw and the kids kept working.

Below, the mothers and babies of the Cradle Roll Department of the First Methodist-Episcopal Church at Two Harbors, Minn., proudly pose for a group picture in 1905.

Courtesy, Mrs. Ruth Locker MacDonald, Two Harbors, Minn.

On the Farm

Although farm machinery had helped speed the shift from subsistence farming to single-crop commercial farming, many an individualistic small farmer found that machines could help him without swamping him. The multiple-disc plough shown *below* did in one operation the work of several, old-style ploughs, and permitted the derby-hatted farmer additional leisure or expansion of activities, as he might choose.

In the picture *below*, a small crew handles the harvest with the aid of a traction-engine, a blower thrasher and an automatic twine-cutter. Notice the belt-transmission in place of the tumbling-rod, the barrels of water for the boiler and the pile of coal in the foreground.

Both illustrations on this page are by the *courtesy* of the J. I. Case Company, Racine, Wis.

Nevada

Through 1905 the mines at Goldfield, and elsewhere in Nevada, continued to flourish. The picture at the *left* shows a pile of sacked ore at the Red Top mine.

The Surveyor General was an important person in a mining state. At the *right* is shown his office in the capitol of Nevada at Carson City. Note the teakettle simmering on the base-burner stove.

Governor Sparks and a party of friends are seen at the *left* as they were leaving Goldfield for the town of Bullfrog, Nev. The date is around 1905.

All illustrations on this page are by the *courtesy* of the Nevada State Historical Society, Reno

City Children

Communities and individuals began to feel a sense of responsibility toward underprivileged children of great cities—like the East Side New Yorkers shown *right*.

Town & Country, May 11, 1907. *Courtesy*, Town & Country, New York City

Courtesy, H. J. Heinz Company, Pittsburgh, Pa.

In Pittsburgh, Pa., a local industry opened a settlement house, as shown *above*, where the energy of youth was directed into learning useful skills and away from breaking windows.

The young Kansas merchant at the *right* worked out his own problems.

Courtesy, "The Jayhawker," University of Kansas, Lawrence

Chain Stores

Two of the practices which established the chain food stores in popular favor are obvious in the 1905 pictures shown *below*.

The use of delivery wagons brought to outlying customers low prices possible through mass purchasing.

The never-failing "something-for-nothing" chord was touched in stores like the Davenport, Iowa, one shown *left*, by distribution of "trading stamps" with each purchase. These were saved and traded in for household utensils, china, etc.

Both illustrations on this page are by the *courtesy* of The Great Atlantic and Pacific Tea Company, New York City

Trends in Advertising

Across Main Street in Richmond, Va., a banner proclaimed the virtues of "My Sweetheart" cigarettes.

Courtesy, The Valentine Museum, Richmond, Va.

Courtesy, The Coca-Cola Company, Atlanta, Ga.

Coca-Cola advertising linked the product with the rising popularity of the automobile. "People who drive cars drink Coca-Cola" was the corollary to the scene *left*.

Quality of the 57 Varieties was proved to the teeth, in the demonstration room shown *below*.

Courtesy, H. J. Heinz Company, Pittsburgh, Pa.

Advertising (*Continued*)

The contrast between styles in the 1907 Goodyear and the 1907 Packard advertisements shown *below* is quite marked. One packs as much copy into the available space as possible. The other simply shows a sketch of next year's model and permits the reader to fill in the blanks with compliments.

The ONLY Rims Requiring "No Tools but the Hands" are **GOODYEAR** UNIVERSAL RIMS Fitted with Goodyear **DETACHABLE AUTO-TIRES**

1.00 pm.

1.01 pm.

1.02 pm.

Off and on again in 60 seconds

ON the road, anywhere, any time of day or night, you can change

... Auto-Rim in a ... the hands. ... ed. Just loosen ... valve stem) and it ... ge rings and off comes ... ge rings and tighten the ... re is on to stay. No strain ... heel to pieces can get it off, till ... sened again. We guarantee that ... n Goodyear Universal Rims can't Rim ... won't replace Rim Cut tires. We do. ... " and "why" at our factory or branches:

... w York, 64th St. and Broadway.   St. Louis, 712-714 Morgan St.
... Francisco, 506 Golden Gate Ave.   Buffalo, 719 Main St.
... cago, 82-84 Michigan Ave.   Detroit, 251 Jefferson Ave.
... veland, 326 Frankfort Ave., N.W.   Pittsburg, 5988 Center Ave.

... booklet, "How to Select an Automobile Tire." It's NOT "mere words." It's ... or you whether you designate our tires and rims or not.

... e & Rubber Co., Detroit St., Akron, Ohio

Harper's Weekly, Nov. 2, 1907
Courtesy, Harper & Brothers, New York City

More and Fertile Eggs

Your hens will positively lay more eggs, and a larger percentage of fertile eggs, if they are given regular doses of Dr. Hess Poultry Pan-a-ce-a with the daily food. It produces this result by the action of bitter tonics which increase the powers of digestion, enabling the system of the fowl to extract the maximum amount of egg-making material from the food and convert it into eggs. It also supplies iron for the blood, and the nitrate to assist nature in expelling poisonous materials through the skin.

DR. HESS POULTRY PAN-A-CE-A

is the prescription of Dr. Hess (M. D., D. V. S.), and besides increasing egg production, it cures and prevents poultry diseases. It contains germicides which destroy bacteria, the cause of nearly all poultry diseases. It has the indorsement of leading Poultry Associations of the United States and Canada. Costs but a penny a day for about 30 fowls, and is sold on a written guarantee.

1½ lbs. 25c, mail or express 40c
5 lbs. 60c
12 lbs. $1.25
25 lb. pail $2.50   } Except in Canada and extreme West and South

Send 2 cents for Dr. Hess 48-page Poultry Book, free.

DR. HESS & CLARK
Ashland, Ohio
Instant Louse Killer
Kills Lice

Courtesy, N. W. Ayer & Son, Inc.,
Philadelphia, Pa.

Above is a 1906 echo from the bucolic past.

Packard "THIRTY" 1908

PACKARD MOTOR CAR COMPANY
DETROIT, MICHIGAN

Harper's Weekly, Dec. 7, 1907
Courtesy, Harper & Brothers, New York City

Furniture

"Grand Rapids" was more than a city in Michigan; it was a symbol. Mass-produced furniture sets for bedroom, dining-room and parlor were the pride of many a humble home, let the aesthetes and the new school of "interior decorators" rage as they might. *Below* are shown a few pieces from Grand Rapids catalogues issued between 1905 and 1907.

All illustrations on this page are from *The Grand Rapids Furniture Record*, 1907. Courtesy, Vincent Edwards Magazines, New York City

Public Servants

Courtesy, Dearborn Historical Commission, Mich.

The Fire Department of Dearborn, Mich., is shown at the *left*.

Detectives of the Baltimore, Md., police department are pictured at work on a difficult case.

Courtesy, J. E. Henry Collection, Enoch Pratt Free Library, Baltimore, Md.

At the *left*, the Regents of Kansas State College are seen discussing the state of education in 1905.

Courtesy, "The Bell-Clapper," Kansas State College, Manhattan

Telephone Goes Underground

Through 1906, progress was made in transferring city telephone cables from the unsightly poles to underground conduits, as seen in the picture *below*.

Before the day of the pneumatic drill, the task of tunnelling through rock was done by hand-drillers. The picture *left* was taken at Eighth Avenue and 36th Street, New York City.

Below, a class of new operators is shown taking instruction at the Telephone Company School, New York City.

All illustrations on this page are by the *courtesy* of the American Telephone and Telegraph Company, New York City

Cut Glass

Every Grand Rapids sideboard was adorned with cut glass bowls, vases, épergnes and pitchers —rarely put to use.

Illustrated World, Technical World, Vol. II, 1904-05
Courtesy, Popular Mechanics, Chicago, Ill.

In the picture of a 1905 glass-blowing plant at the *left*, the men are giving initial form to the molten glass from the furnace.

At the *right*, a workman cuts the design on a vase.

Illustrated World, Technical World, Vol. II, 1904-05
Courtesy, Popular Mechanics, Chicago, Ill.

Below are shown some of the cut glass patterns for 1905.

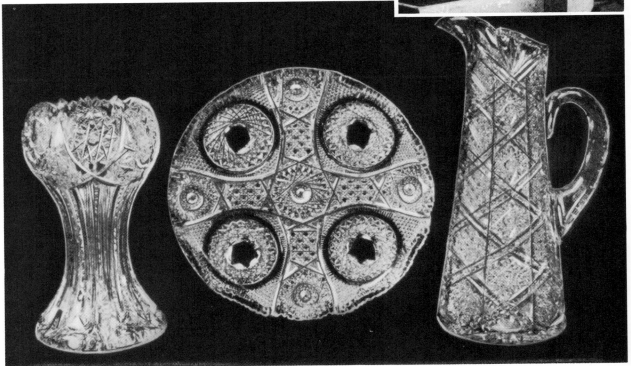

Harper's Bazar, May, 1905. Courtesy, Harper's Bazaar, New York City

Insurance

From Sept. 6, 1905, to the end of that year, Charles Evans Hughes made a national reputation by his pitiless exposure of the practices of great American insurance companies and their exploitation and waste of policy-holders' money entrusted to them.

The extravagance of a costume ball given at Sherry's on the night of Jan. 31, 1905, by the head of one of the companies first drew public attention to what was to prove a sensational scandal. *Above,* a group of the "younger set" are practicing a figure for the ball. *Below,* Madame Réjane (an ornament of the French stage imported for the occasion) steps out of a sedan-chair for the Versailles Pageant presented at the party.

Both illustrations on this page are from the Byron Collection, *courtesy,* Museum of the City of New York

Schools

Near Arnhold's Mill, Mo., the patriarchal master of the three "R's" shown at the *left* presided over all grades.

Courtesy, Charles van Ravenswaay Collection, Missouri Historical Society, St. Louis

Below, a kindergarten group is seen in Monroe Park, Richmond, Va.

Courtesy, The Valentine Museum, Richmond, Va.

The Private School

At the *right*, crew candidates at St. Paul's School clutter up Long Pond, Concord, N. H.

Town & Country, Aug. 20, 1904. *Courtesy*, Town & Country, New York City

Women's Colleges

Each returning spring brought its graduation pageantry. At the *left*, the Wellesley seniors of 1906 go to bid farewell to their tree. *Below*, hard-working Vassar sophomores of the same year bear the Daisy Chain.

Town & Country, Aug. 18, 1906.
Courtesy, Town & Country, New York City

Town & Country, Aug. 18, 1906. *Courtesy*, Town & Country, New York City

College and College Men

The books so avidly studied by men of the Senior Debating Society at Kansas State College (shown at the *left*) were copies of *Roberts' Rules of Order*.

Courtesy, "The Bell-Clapper," Kansas State College, Manhattan

The 1907 advertisement from a college publication seen at the *right* set a fast sartorial pace.

We Want You to See Our

STEDWOR CLOTHES

Made by a concern in the East that makes only *best* men's clothing. A concern that keeps abreast of the tailors instead of getting style changes six months late.

And the fabrics?

Beauties! You'd have to pay half more to get a tailor to put such distinctive materials into a suit. Let us show them to you the next time your in town.

$15, $16.50, $18, and $20

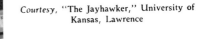

12th, Main and Walnut Streets   KANSAS CITY, MISSOURI

Courtesy, "The Jayhawker," University of Kansas, Lawrence

Note in this 1906 picture of a student's room at Princeton, the bric-a-brac, the "Morris" chair and the Gibson Girl prints on the wall.

Courtesy, Princeton University Library and R. C. Rose and Son, Princeton, N. J.

West Point

The new, dynamic foreign policy of the United States looked to its service schools for intelligent support. The Army did not lag behind the Navy in modernizing and improving its educational program.

Town & Country, June 16, 1906
Courtesy, Town & Country, New York City

But regardless of changes in theory and curriculum, inspection (*above*) was still a cadet ordeal. Occasionally an Academy social function, like the garden party shown *left*, broke in on the grind.

Town & Country, May 30, 1908
Courtesy, Town & Country, New York City

To the Pole

At the *right*, Commander Robert E. Peary is shown with his sailing master aboard the auxiliary schooner *Roosevelt*, as he talks over his 1905 try for the North Pole.

Harper's Weekly, July 22, 1905
Courtesy, Harper & Brothers, New York City

Art

Some American artists of the early Nineteen Hundreds employed the technique of the French Impressionists in their studies of the American scene.

The painting at the *left*, by E. C. Tarbell, depicted a Boston living-room of about 1907, complete with Winthrop desk and Japanese prints.

Courtesy, The Corcoran Gallery of Art, Washington, D. C.

John Singer Sargent's great portrait-group of the "Four Doctors" was unveiled at Johns Hopkins University in January, 1907. The doctors are William H. Welch, William Osler, William S. Halsted and Howard A. Kelly.

Courtesy, The Johns Hopkins University, Baltimore, Md.

John Sloan caught in his "Wake of the Ferry" (*left*) the mood of a dull day in New York harbor.

Courtesy, Phillips Memorial Gallery, Washington, D. C.

Popular Art

Popular illustrators rang the changes on a subject of perennial fascination—the pretty American girl.

The 1905 girl is shown at the *right* as she was seen by Harrison Fisher. *Below,* she is seen as J. C. Leyendecker sketched her.

Scribner's Magazine, June, 1905

Scribner's Magazine, July, 1905

In 1907, James Montgomery Flagg drew the pretty girl on tour, shown *right*.

The gentlemen in all three pictures were properly incidental.

Scribner's Magazine, August, 1907

Broadway: 1905

Harper's Weekly, May 27, 1905
Courtesy, Harper & Brothers, New York City

The New York Hippodrome was offering "A Yankee Circus on Mars." At the *left* is shown the Dance of the Hours from that masterpiece.

The ever-beautiful Lillian Russell appeared in a musical version of the "School for Scandal" as Lady Teazle *(right)*.

Town & Country, Mar. 30, 1907
Courtesy, Town & Country, New York City

Anna Held opened at the Knickerbocker in "Mam'selle Napoleon." At the *left* is a scene from Act I.

Robinson Locke Collection
Courtesy, The New York Public Library, New York City

Broadway: 1906-1907

Town & Country, Apr. 6, 1907. *Courtesy*, Town & Country, New York City

"The Parisian Model" at the Broadway Theater took occasion of the latest fad to present a Teddy Bear Chorus (*above*). A once-famous cartoon on President Roosevelt's big-game hunting started the vogue for Teddy Bears.

The playbill to the *right* explains itself.

Town & Country, Mar. 24, 1906
Courtesy, Town & Country, New York City

Maude Adams, *above*, was memorable as "Peter Pan."

JARDIN DE PARIS
(THE GARDEN OF PARIS)
ATOP THE NEW YORK AND CRITERION THEATRES,
Broadway from 14th Street to 45th Street.

MANAGEMENT OF F. ZIEGFELD, JR.

WEEK BEGINNING MONDAY EVENING, JULY 22, 1907.
Every Evening, Commencing at 8.30

1 OVERTURE . . . . Jardin de Paris Orchestra

2 SELECTION . . . . "Follies of 1907"

The ZIEGFELD Musical Revue,

3 **FOLLIES OF 1907**
1 2 3 4 5 6 7   8 9   10 11 12 13
Another One of Those Things, in Thirteen Acts.
Conceived and Produced by F. ZIEGFELD, JR.
Words by Harry B. Smith. Music and Lyrics by Everybody.
Principals Directed by Mr. Herbert Gresham.
Chorus Directed by Mr. Julian Mitchell.
Frederick Solomon, Musical Director.

The novelties and acts devised for this entertainment by Mr. F. Ziegfeld, Jr.,
have been copyrighted and protected to the full extent of the law, and the per-
forming rights of all are restricted. Anyone using them or any managers
allowing them to be performed in their theatres, will be prosecuted.
All songs restricted.

Courtesy, Museum of the City of New York

Ethel Barrymore appeared in "The Silver Box," by John Galsworthy. She is seen *below* in the trial scene from that play.

Town & Country, Apr. 6, 1907. *Courtesy*, Town & Country, New York City

Minor Theater

Courtesy, Scribner Art File

The "nickelodeon" days of the motion-picture are typified in the picture at the *left*, taken on New York's East Side around 1906.

"Joe Joker," the wonder horse who ran against time without driver, sulky or hobbles, was a star attraction at State Fairs.

Courtesy, Mr. Myron F. Henkel, Springfield, Ill.

At Luna Park, Coney Island, the big show for 1907 was "The Days of Forty-Nine," shown *left*. There was a creek with real water through which the stagecoach splashed, and ears rang with the roar of .44 Colts in expert (?) hands.

Town & Country, Aug. 3, 1907. *Courtesy,* Town & Country, New York City

The Common Touch

Americans enjoyed non-exclusive group activities of all kinds, sponsored as a rule by churches or clubs.

Participants in a 1905 crab feast at Back River, Md., are seen at the *right*.

Courtesy, J. E. Henry Collection, Enoch Pratt Free Library, Baltimore, Md.

The Tally-Ho excursion shown *below* set off for Milwaukee from Ravenswood, Ill., on Aug. 11, 1907.

Courtesy, Ravenswood-Lake View Historical Association, sponsored by The Chicago Public Library, Ill.

How to Pass a Summer Day

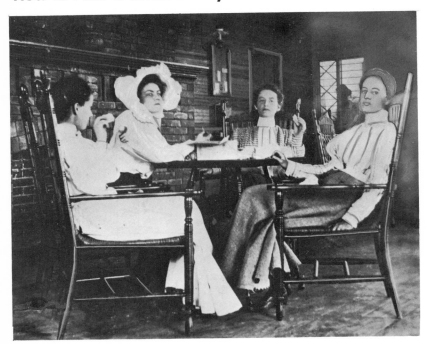

Courtesy, Mr. Myron F. Henkel, Springfield, Ill.

The "new woman" wound up a leisurely round of golf with lunch at the club-house as seen *left* in a 1905 picture from Springfield, Ill.

But under the watchful eye of the old first sergeant behind the gun, these ladies of the older school amused themselves with a walk through the grounds of the Soldiers' Home.

Courtesy, Mr. Stephen L. Newnham, Philadelphia, Pa.

Patriotic Occasions

The Fourth of July, 1906, was observed in San Mateo, Calif., with the parade shown at the *right*.

Courtesy, San Mateo County Historical Association, San Mateo, Calif.

In a Chicago suburb, celebration of the glorious Fourth was a community affair, opened with a formal flag-raising at the local club.

Courtesy, Ravenswood-Lake View Historical Association, sponsored by The Chicago Public Library, Ill.

As shown at the *right*, a parade through the streets of Richmond, Va., preceded the unveiling of a monument to General J. E. B. Stuart.

Courtesy, The Valentine Museum, Richmond, Va.

Folk-Lore of Motoring

Courtesy, Mr. Myron F. Henkel, Springfield, Ill.

Get out and get under is exemplified at the *left* in a 1905 picture taken on the road to Clear Lake, near Springfield, Ill. The driver is on the far side of the car, making "slight, mechanical adjustments."

Pull over to the curb! as it was ordered in Detroit, Mich., some time around 1906, is recalled in the picture at the *right*.

Courtesy, Detroit Public Library, Mich.

Let me teach you to drive. It's easy.

At the *left*, the consequences of such lightly-uttered words are seen.

Harper's Weekly, Mar. 24, 1906. Courtesy, Harper & Brothers, New York City

Pride of Possession

Ownership of a motor-car in 1906 carried with it a certain *éclat*. In the picture *below*, the celebrated actress Rose Melville, "Sis Hopkins," enjoys the feel of her Pope-Hartford.

Photo by W. H. Bass Co., Indianapolis, Ind. *Courtesy*, The Indiana Historical Society, Indianapolis

And Mr. Goldstein himself posed proudly at the wheel of his brand-new 1906 Mack truck.

Courtesy, Mack-International Motor Truck Corporation, New York City

Transport by Motor

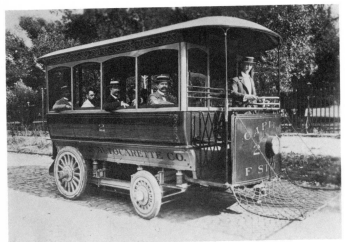

Courtesy, American Car and Foundry Company, New York City

The "autocarette" shown *left* operated in Washington, D. C.

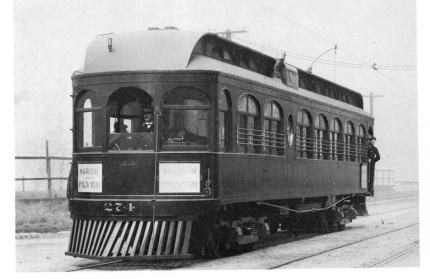

Photo by W. H. Bass Co., Indianapolis, Ind.
Courtesy, The Indiana Historical Society, Indianapolis

Between towns and cities in the Midwest, "interurban" lines like the one shown *right* cut deep into steam railroad passenger traffic.

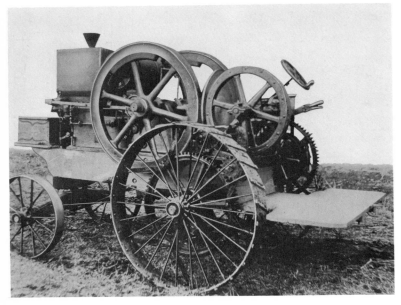

Courtesy, International Harvester Company, Chicago, Ill.

Around 1905, the experimental motor tractor shown *left* foreshadowed a new era for the small farmer.

Panama Canal

President Roosevelt ended all political difficulties in the way of a canal across the Isthmus of Panama by encouraging a Panamanian revolution against the Republic of Colombia, then recognizing the insurgent government and accepting its offer of a special zone across the Isthmus. Construction had been begun in 1904. By 1905, many technical difficulties were being encountered.

French engineers had already failed to overcome the sanitary and engineering problems involved. Some of the abandoned French equipment is shown at the *right.*

Illustrated World, Technical World, Vol. I, 1904
Courtesy, Popluar Mechanics, Chicago, Ill.

Tropical rains caused washouts and wrecks.

Harper's Weekly, Dec. 9, 1905. *Courtesy,* Harper & Brothers, New York City

After Dr. William Gorgas was given authority to develop a campaign against yellow fever and malaria among the workmen, greater progress was made. At the *right,* the hospital at Ancon Hill is shown.

Harper's Weekly, Dec. 9, 1905. *Courtesy,* Harper & Brothers, New York City

The Chicago Stock Yards

To the President's friends, they stood for loathesome working conditions and unsanitary practices which he had countered with his Meat Inspection Law of 1906: To the President's foes they stood for a battleground of private enterprise against political opportunism.

From a photo by William H. Jackson
Courtesy, Scribner Art File

Harper's Weekly, Feb. 2, 1907
Courtesy, Harper & Brothers, New York City

Reclamation

of arid land went on apace. *Above*, the Laguna Dam on the Colorado River is shown as it looked in 1906.

Burbank

Out in California, Luther Burbank was becoming a household name for his hybrid species of fruit. At the *left*, he is seen in the center of the group, at work on a giant pie-plant.

W. S. Harwood, *New Creations in Plant Life*. 1905
Courtesy, The Macmillan Company, New York City

San Francisco Tragedy

Early in the morning of Apr. 18, 1906, a series of heavy earthquake shocks hit San Francisco and a wide area about the city. For three days, fire raged uncontrolled and about a third of the city was razed.

At the *right* is shown a view of the stricken city taken through the ruins of a doorway on the hill. The City Hall, seen in the distance, is shown in close-up *below*, its steel skeleton stripped of masonry by the shocks.

Courtesy, California Historical Society, San Francisco

Harper's Weekly, May 5, 1906
Courtesy, Harper & Brothers, New York City

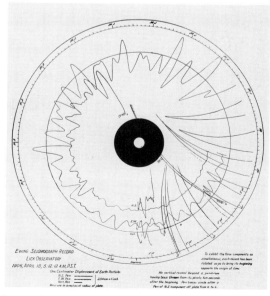

At the *right* is a reproduction of the seismograph record from Lick Observatory. Ten seconds after the beginning of the earthquake, the pendulum was thrown from its pivots.

Courtesy, Lick Observatory, Mount Hamilton, Calif.

San Francisco Tragedy (Continued)

Ruptured gas mains quickly caught fire, and failure of water by reason of broken lines made it necessary to fight the fire with dynamite. The convulsive force of the earthquake is readily appreciated in the picture *above*.

Survivors did not stay for long passive as in the picture *below*. Order was restored, looting severely punished and a new San Francisco began to rise.

Both illustrations on this page are by the *courtesy* of the California Historical Society, San Francisco

New York Slums

For many years the seamier side of New York life had been played down in view of the city's increasing wealth. Reformers and social workers, however, were by 1906 making their appeals to the conscience of the general public, and political repercussions followed.

Harper's Weekly, Apr. 28, 1906. *Courtesy*, Harper & Brothers, New York City

The picture *above* shows a street in the notorious "Tenderloin" district — the prey of grafting policemen and criminals.

Some of the Chinese who lived on squalid lower Mott Street, Pell and Doyers Streets (*right*), engaged in numerous private wars between family associations or "tongs."

Harper's Weekly, Aug. 17, 1907
Courtesy, Harper & Brothers, New York City

In the News

Harper's Weekly, Mar. 3, 1906
Courtesy, Harper & Brothers, New York City

On Saturday, Feb. 17, 1906, the crowd shown *left* had gathered to watch the guests arriving for the marriage of "Princess Alice" Roosevelt to Representative Nicholas Longworth in the East Room of the White House.

August Post and Charles Glidden are shown at the start of the 1906 "Glidden Tour," from Buffalo, N. Y., to Bretton Woods, N. H. These "reliability runs" were important in popularizing auto touring and stressing the need for better roads.

Harper's Weekly, July 28, 1906
Courtesy, Harper & Brothers, New York City

Assorted Riots

Harper's Weekly, Aug. 25, 1906.   Courtesy, Harper & Brothers, New York City

During the early summer of 1906, the Brooklyn Rapid Transit Company doubled the fare to Coney Island, in violation of a Supreme Court injunction. The picture *above* shows police restraining protesting Brooklynites at the point where the double fare was collected.

The trial of Bill Haywood and other officers of the Western Federation of Miners at Boise City, Idaho, for the murder of ex-Governor Frank Steunenberg, had repercussions all through the nation as labor groups protested President Roosevelt's denunciation of the men. *Below* is shown a demonstration in New York.

Harper's Weekly, May 18, 1907. Courtesy, Harper & Brothers, New York City

Great Outdoors

The National Parks attracted increasing numbers of vacationing visitors. President Roosevelt's enthusiasm for the "great outdoors" was contagious.

Yancey's Stage Station near Tower Falls in Yellowstone Park is seen at the *left* as it looked in 1905. Over the dusty roads, there came to it stages full of tourists like the one shown *below*.

Courtesy, National Park Service

Courtesy, National Park Service

With a trophy of his keen eye and straight-shooting rifle, the President is seen *left*. His penchant for bears has already been noticed on page 237.

Scribner's Magazine, November, 1905

Conservation Crusade Continues

In February, 1907, the President recommended once again an organized program for conservation of natural resources. But the approach was more emotional than scientific.

Pictures like the view of Wisconsin stump land at the *right* were circulated to highlight the waste of lumbering operations.

Illustrated World, Technical World, Vol. II, 1904-05
Courtesy, Popular Mechanics, Chicago, Ill.

Courtesy, Minnesota Historical Society, St. Paul

But the stubbornly destructive (and picturesque) industry continued its old practices.

At the *left* is shown a driving crew at work on a jam above Chippewa Falls, Wis.

Some Wisconsin lumberjacks are seen at the *right* in their bunk-room. The picture dates from about 1905.

Courtesy, Minnesota Historical Society, St. Paul

Balloon Race

Hailed as "the greatest event yet, in the history of aeronautics," the 1907 race for the Gordon Bennett cup was won by the German entry "Pommern." Five dirigibles entered in the contest. The start was made from St. Louis, Mo., as shown in the view *below*.

Courtesy, Missouri Historical Society, St. Louis

Lincoln Beachey is seen at the *left*, taking off in one of the dirigibles.

Popular Mechanics, December, 1907
Courtesy, Popular Mechanics, Chicago, Ill.

Panic of 1907

For more than a year, interest on short term loans had been fluctuating between ten and one-hundred-and-twenty-five per cent. Experienced bankers were expecting a currency panic and it came on Oct. 21, 1907, with a failure of public confidence in the ability of banks to meet obligations.

The Knickerbocker Trust Company of New York was the first victim. As police controlled the anxious depositors waiting to withdraw their cash (*right*), the bank officials tried to borrow cash in order to meet the drain.

Harper's Weekly, Nov. 9, 1907
Courtesy, Harper & Brothers, New York City

Since each bank stood alone in 1907, support from other banks was a matter of good will. There was no national banking system.

With the suspension of payment by many banks, Wall Street ceased trading and the Street filled with anxious crowds (*left*). In home neighborhoods, branches of banks were in a state of siege (*below*).

Harper's Weekly, Nov. 9, 1907
Courtesy, Harper & Brothers, New York City

Scrip was issued in lieu of pay checks; the President blamed the crisis on "malefactors of great wealth"; J. P. Morgan rallied the money forces and restored public confidence.

W. H. Hillyer, *James Talcott: Merchant*. 1937

The Peace Doves Sail

American interference in the Russo-Japanese War, and recent Japanese exclusion legislation had stirred up anti-American feeling in Nippon. President Roosevelt felt that the Oriental mind might be inclined more toward peace if the United States battle fleet paid a friendly call to Eastern waters. In December, 1907, sixteen battleships sailed from Hampton Roads under Admiral "Fighting Bob" Evans—destination, San Francisco and the Pacific.

Harper's Weekly, Dec. 7, 1907. *Courtesy*, Harper & Brothers, New York City

Harper's Weekly, Dec. 28, 1907
Courtesy, Harper & Brothers, New York City

In the picture *above*, components of the fleet are being prepared at Brooklyn Navy Yard for the long voyage. In the foreground is the *West Virginia*.

At the *left*, the flag-ship *Connecticut* is shown as she got under way.

8

A CHANGE OF HORSES

Economic consequences of the 1907 financial panic were felt in the ensuing year.

The Illinois "toggery shop" at the *right* was one of many small businesses with full stocks and low sales.

Courtesy, Mr. Myron F. Henkel, Springfield, Ill.

Unemployed men and boys studied the "Help Wanted" pages of the newspapers. The picture *below* was taken in City Hall Park, New York City.

Courtesy, Consolidated Edison Company of New York, Inc., New York City

Steel

The United States Steel Corporation continued to prosper and expand in this heyday of heavy metal, despite the growth of a strong public sentiment against its size and monopolistic character.

At the *left* is shown an ore freighter loading iron ore at Duluth in 1909.

Courtesy, St. Louis County Historical Society, Duluth, Minn.

Gary

There were three reasons why the Steel Corporation raised a city on a waste shore, twenty-six miles southeast of Chicago. It provided an exclusive Great Lakes port; its rail facilities were perfect; it was closer to the sources of ore than older steel cities. At the *right* is seen Gary, Ind., under construction in 1907.

Courtesy, Scribner Art File

At the other end of town, the residential section was planned and administered by the Corporation. The workmen's houses shown *left* rented for sixteen dollars a month in 1908.

Harper's Weekly, July 4, 1908. *Courtesy,* Harper & Brothers, New York City

Votes for Women

The reform atmosphere engendered by President Theodore Roosevelt encouraged fighters for women's rights to renew their struggle in 1908.

"Foreign agitators" helped boil the pot. At the *right*, Mrs. Cobden Sanderson, a leader of English suffragettes, is shown speaking at Labor Hall, New York City.

Harper's Weekly, Jan. 18, 1908
Courtesy, Harper & Brothers, New York City

Harper's Weekly, Jan. 18, 1908
Courtesy, Harper & Brothers, New York City

At the *left*, Mrs. Borrman Wells, another embattled British feminist, is seen addressing an open-air meeting in Madison Square, New York City.

A mass demonstration of suffragettes in New York, late in February, 1908, was gently but firmly discouraged by the police. At the *right*, Mrs. Wells and Miss Maud Malone (left foreground) are being "moved on."

Harper's Weekly, Mar. 7, 1908
Courtesy, Harper & Brothers, New York City

Prohibition

The drive against liquor had become by 1908 a moral crusade of disconcerting power.

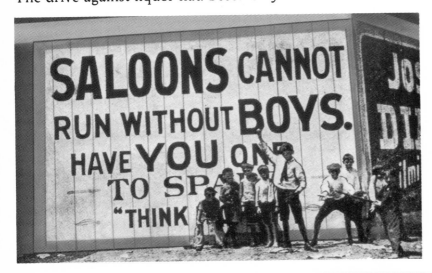

Courtesy, Scribner Art File

Signboards like the one shown *left* preached silent sermons, usually in close proximity to beer and whiskey advertisements.

The man at the wheel in the picture *right* was W. E. (Pussyfoot) Johnson, scourge of the booze peddlers and once a household name.

Harper's Weekly, Feb. 26, 1910
Courtesy, Harper & Brothers, New York City

The State of Maine had tried to enforce its pioneer prohibition statutes, long nullified in fact; but in January, 1909, the Maine saloon shown *left* was still operating defiantly, and all that had been achieved was a split in the local Republican Party.

Harper's Weekly, Feb. 6, 1909
Courtesy, Harper & Brothers, New York City

On the Boards

Rising costs and the tight hold on the entertainment industry exercised by the "Theater Trust" were bringing about vast changes in the American theater.

"Girlie shows" like those advertised at the *right* were expensive to produce and could afford to play only the larger cities.

Courtesy, The Managing Editor

Local "opry houses" like the Bradley in Fort Edward, N. Y., shown *left*, housed an occasional "Tom Show" and paid the interest on the mortgage with the rent from the penny arcade and nickelodeon downstairs. It was the end of the "road."

ourtesy, Fort Edward Public Library and Stone Studio, Fort Edward, N. Y.

In July, 1908, the picture at the *right* was taken at an actors' picnic. Left to right stand three veterans of the older stage : Tom Lewis, Lew Dockstader the Minstrel, and Tony Pastor.

Harper's Weekly, Sept. 5, 1908
Courtesy, Harper & Brothers, New York City

Stage in 1908

The veteran actor of the Yiddish theater, Jacob Adler, appeared in "King Lear." *Below* is shown the Grand Street Theater, New York City, where his English début took place.

Courtesy, Byron Collection, Museum of the City of New York

George Ade's "Fair Co-Ed" carried on the college-boy-baiting spirit of the "College Widow." The picture of the 1908 production *below* shows Elsie Janis at the front and center.

Courtesy, Purdue University, Lafayette, Ind.

Olympic Victory

Athletes from the United States led the nearest competition by forty-eight and one-third points at London Stadium in July, 1908.

At the *right*, A. C. Gilbert of Yale tops the wood in the pole vault at twelve feet, two inches.

Harper's Weekly, Aug. 1, 1908
Courtesy, Harper & Brothers, New York City

When the winners returned, New York City turned out to welcome them. The parade is seen at the *left* as it passed Madison Square on Aug. 29, 1908.

Part of the reception at City Hall is shown *below*. The standing figure is J. J. Hayes, winner of the disputed Marathon run.

Harper's Weekly, Sept. 5, 1908
Courtesy, Harper & Brothers, New York City

Harper's Weekly, Sept. 5, 1908. Courtesy, Harper & Brothers, New York City

Flight

At Fort Myer, Va., on Sept. 9, 1908, Orville Wright flew his plane continuously for fifty-seven minutes thirty-one seconds, at a speed of thirty-five miles an hour.

The picture *left* shows Orville Wright as he was achieving the then world's record for flight in a heavier than air machine.

Photo by United States Signal Corps
Courtesy, Scribner Art File

In late May of the same year, C. A. Morrell's dirigible had collapsed and fallen on its trial flight as shown in the picture at the *right*, taken just as the bag ruptured.

Popular Mechanics, July, 1908
Courtesy, Popular Mechanics, Chicago, Ill.

Wilbur Kimball's 1908 heliocopter (shown *left*) caused Thomas Edison to proclaim it the "aeroplane of the future."

Popular Mechanics, December, 1908
Courtesy, Popular Mechanics, Chicago, Ill.

Naval Emphasis

The United States was not lagging in the international race for sea-power. First American "Dreadnought" class battleship was the *North Dakota*, launched in November, 1908. Submarines were not neglected.

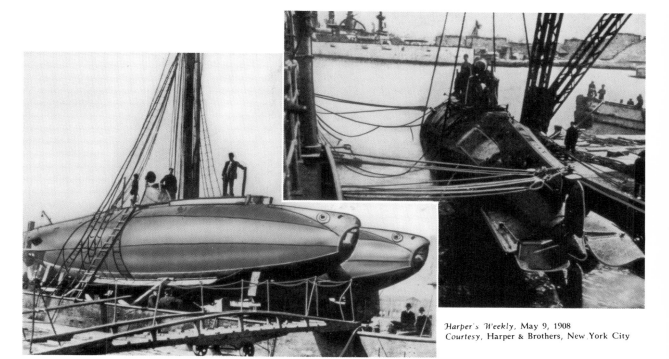

Harper's Weekly, May 9, 1908. Courtesy, Harper & Brothers, New York City

Harper's Weekly, May 9, 1908
Courtesy, Harper & Brothers, New York City

Shark and *Porpoise* nest side by side on the deck of a transport vessel in the picture *above*.

Above, a submarine is being hoisted aboard a collier at Brooklyn Navy Yard for shipment to Manila, P. I.

At the *right*, *Tarpon* is launched in April, 1909, at Quincy, Mass.

Popular Mechanics, June, 1908. Courtesy, Popular Mechanics, Chicago, Ill.

A Mild Campaign

Theodore Roosevelt hand-picked his successor as Republican candidate for the Presidency. His loyal, genial Secretary of War, William Howard Taft, was the man who could be trusted to carry on the Roosevelt policies. His fine record of public service was eloquent in his favor.

Taft and J. S. Sherman, candidate for Vice-President, are seen at the *left*, as they arrived at Cincinnati, Ohio, after leaving the Chicago convention.

Harper's Weekly, July 4, 1908. *Courtesy*, Harper & Brothers, New York City

At Denver, Colo., William Jennings Bryan dictated his own renomination as Democratic candidate. After the fiasco of 1904, the delegates had no choice. In the picture *below*, Bryan is shown "accepting" the nomination on the steps of the Capitol, Lincoln, Neb.

Harper's Weekly, Aug. 29, 1908. *Courtesy*, Harper & Brothers, New York City

A Mild Campaign (*Continued*)

To the man in the street, the differences between platforms of the parties seemed academic. Taft was elected President by 321 electoral votes to Bryan's 162; the Republicans took a majority in both houses of Congress. But not before—

Bryan had shaken hands with Boss Murphy of Tammany Hall, as seen at the *right*.

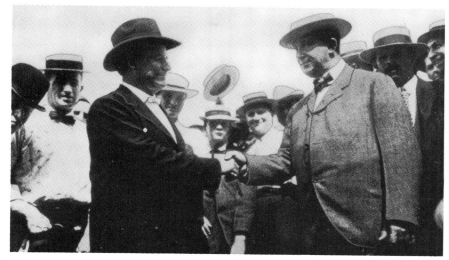

Harper's Weekly, July 25, 1908. Courtesy, Harper & Brothers, New York City

Taft had displayed unsuspected talents as a baby-kisser. (The incident *left* took place at Sandusky, Ohio.)

Harper's Weekly, Sept. 26, 1908. Courtesy, Harper & Brothers, New York City

And Eugene V. Debs aboard "The Red Special" (*right*, at Waterbury, Conn.) had toured industrial cities of the East with his Socialist denunciations of the senior parties.

Harper's Weekly, Oct. 17, 1908. Courtesy, Harper & Brothers, New York City

The People

The new President was not given to generalizing men and women into "the people," a unitary mass for which something had to be done. In an honest endeavor to understand the diversity of American character which lay beyond his urban experience, he toured the country.

He might have seen in rural North Carolina the Monday morning "washday" ritual at the *left*.

Courtesy, North Carolina State Department of Archives and History, Raleigh

Or the Croatoan Indians shown *right* outside their North Carolina cabin.

Courtesy, North Carolina State Department of Archives and History, Raleigh

To the north and west at Eagle Rapids, Wis., he might have visited the hard-working group shown *left* on the deck of the *Dancing Annie*, supply boat for a lumber camp.

Courtesy, Minnesota Historical Society, St. Paul

The Farmer

But the charming, jovial Taft did not get to meet the people he should have met. "Important" persons diverted him from the grass-roots people shown *below*, whose loyalties still lay with the Republican party.

From the North Dakota wheat farmers (*above*, loading bundles; *below*, ploughing stubble) he might have learned that agriculture was beginning to question the wisdom of Republican policies.

Both illustrations on this page are by the *courtesy* of the Great Northern Railway Company, St. Paul, Minn.

America the Unbeautiful

Without design or plan beyond the imperative of the real estate speculator, the cities of the United States had continued to sprawl farther and farther out from their original centers.

Courtesy, Consolidated Edison Company of New York, Inc., New York City

Upper Broadway, New York City (*left*), had developed by 1908 at the expense of former "downtown" residential areas which in many cases were fast becoming slums.

The billboards which decorated Broad Street, Richmond, Va. (*right*), were becoming a blight along country roads as well. The auto tourist made his way between walls of shrieking ads.

Courtesy, The Valentine Museum, Richmond, Va.

The average citizen of Tacoma, Wash. (*left*), felt that the Northern Pacific yards in the foreground did more for him than the view of Mount Rainier.

Harper's Weekly, Apr. 3, 1909. *Courtesy,* Harper & Brothers, New York City

Family Life

As yet, few fashionable innovations in family organization and discipline had filtered down to the average family.

Courtesy, Associate Editor

The Columbus, Ohio, family *above* believed in the solid virtues of loyalty, co-operation and forbearance.

The evening "at home" in Chicago, pictured *below*, was possible in the days before cheap motorcars and the "movies" altered traditional ways.

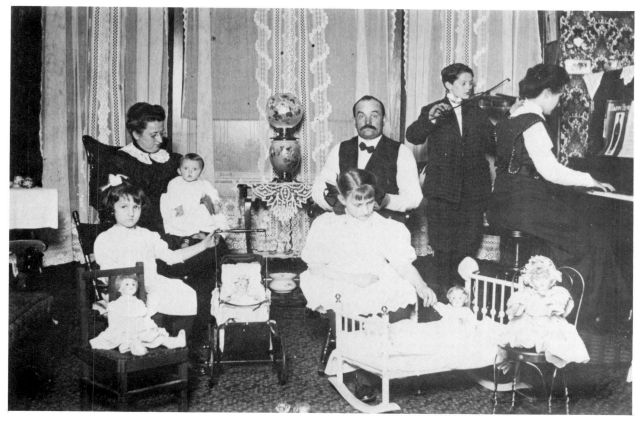

Courtesy, Chicago Lawn Historical Society and Chicago Public Library, Ill.

Furniture

The three "parlor suites" shown *below* were standard equipment for the average home of 1908-1909.

At the *left* is a nondescript parlor-library set in mahogany.

The influence of the fashionable decorator is seen in the catalogue illustrations *right* and *below*. At the *right* is a "colonial" set: *Below* is the magnificence of Louis Quinze —at a price.

All illustrations on this page are from *The Grand Rapids Furniture Record*, 1908. Courtesy, Vincent Edwards Magazines, New York City

Sunday Clothes

At the *right*, is what happened when lively, little New York boys were taken to have their pictures made.

Although Paris had decreed otherwise for the fashionable, an average American family would have arrayed itself for a Sunday outing in the style of the Chicago family shown *below*.

Courtesy, Associate Editor

Courtesy, Chicago Lawn Historical Society and Chicago Public Library, Ill.

Relaxation

Buffalo Bill *The Annie*

From The Alfred E. Smith Collection
Courtesy, Museum of the City of New York

The photo-postcard at the *left*, showing Alfred E. Smith as *Annie Oakley* and Judge James Hoyer as *Buffalo Bill*, was sent to Mrs. Smith from the 1908 Democratic Convention at Denver, Colo.

Below is seen one of the 1908 activities of the Women's Club of San Mateo, Calif. The higher seriousness and lecture-mindedness of women's clubs came at a later date.

Courtesy, San Mateo County Historical Association, San Mateo, Calif.

Billy Sunday

The big-league ballplayer turned evangelist was at the height of his career in 1908.

The picture at the *right* shows Sunday (second from the left) and members of his party as he arrived for a two-month revival in Springfield, Ill.

In a specially built tabernacle on the northwest corner of First and Adams streets, he addressed meetings like the one shown *below*. This picture was taken from the rear of the auditorium on Mar. 7, 1909.

Both illustrations on this page are by the *courtesy* of Mr. Myron F. Henkel, Springfield, Ill.

The Humble

Not all Americans were successful, energetic and optimistic. There were some who served in patience.

Courtesy, North Carolina State Department of Archives and History, Raleigh

Aunt Dolly, *left*, had nursed four generations of a North Carolina family.

The elderly lady *below* was pictured at her post of duty in a Chicago suburb.

The wandering scissors-grinder shouldered his wheel and rang his bell from town to town.

The two lower pictures, *Courtesy*, Chicago Lawn Historical Society and Chicago Public Library, Ill.

Education

Many onerous parts of the child-rearing process were being absorbed into public education by progressive teachers and school administrators. *Below*, a school nurse teaches Cincinnati children how to brush their teeth.

L. W. Rapeer, ed., *Educational Hygiene.* 1915

Below is shown the chemistry laboratory at Two Harbors, Minn., High School. Technical training was useful; therefore it was good and was rapidly pushing out the older classical curriculum.

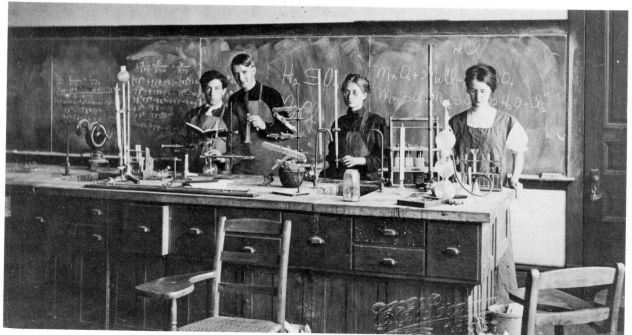

Courtesy, Mrs. Ruth Locker MacDonald, Two Harbors, Minn.

Advertising

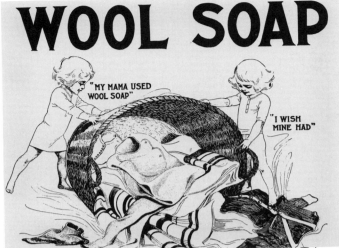

Courtesy, Swift & Company, Chicago, Ill.

Advertising continued to play to a mass audience with carefully chosen symbols. At the *left* are the famous Wool Soap children.

Courtesy, N. W. Ayer & Son, Inc., Philadelphia, Pa.

The three "modish figures" in the advertisement at the *right* gave each feminine reader an idea of the way she might look —if.

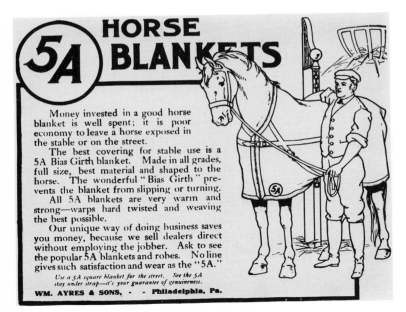

Courtesy, N. W. Ayer & Son, Inc., Philadelphia, Pa.

A somewhat similar claim was made for the "Bias Girth" blanket advertised at the *left*.

Famous Firsts in Motoring

The Ford Model "T" of 1908 is shown at the *right*.

Courtesy, Ford Motor Company, Dearborn, Mich.

Harper's Weekly, Feb. 1, 1908. Courtesy, Harper & Brothers, New York City

Propagandists for the motor industry were stressing the "dependability" of automobiles. In February, 1908, the new, demountable-rim tire was a factor in this campaign. At the *left*, a motorist changes a blown tire "easily and quickly" by the new method.

The picture *right* purports to show "the first horseless funeral in the United States." In May, 1910, Henry Stephens of Detroit was the occasion of this event. It was noted that "good, fast time was made from the house to the cemetery."

Harper's Weekly, June 4, 1910. Courtesy, Harper & Brothers, New York City

Out For a Spin

Courtesy, Managing Editor

Above, a Kansas couple try out their brand-new 1909 Buick. Mother is obviously pleased with the effect on the neighbors.

An early specimen of a new industry is pictured *below*: the first garage in Hempstead, N. Y.

Courtesy, The Hempstead Library, Hempstead, N. Y.

Trucks

By 1910, the motor-truck was accepted for all kinds of haulage.

The International auto-wagon *right* worked on a farm.

Courtesy, International Harvester Company, Chicago, Ill.

Courtesy, Mack-International Motor Truck Corporation, New York City

Express companies overcame the prejudice in favor of horses for short hauls. Note in the picture *left* that one of the Mack trucks has its wheel at the right-hand side.

Coca-Cola distributed its product by motor-truck in Hamlet, N. C., as seen in the picture at the *right*. Note the French horn.

Courtesy, The Coca-Cola Company, Atlanta, Ga.

Vanishing Americana

Curtesy, H. J. Heinz Company, Pittsburgh, Pa.

As late as 1909, the older generation of brewers and merchants entered "Blue Ribbon" teams like the one shown *above* in prize competitions.

The queens of the Mississippi still put in at Bienville Street wharf, New Orleans.

Courtesy, Board of Commissioners of the Port of New Orleans, La.

Firemen

The small boy of 1909 could thrill to the sight shown *right*. But in the 1910 view of part of the Baltimore, Md., Fire Department *below*, the chief's car and one engine were motorized.

Courtesy, The Home Insurance Company, New York City

Courtesy, The Municipal Museum of the City of Baltimore, Md.

Better Roads

The Glidden Tours; the automobile manufacturers; an aroused public spirit, all aided in the continued improvement of highways and secondary roads.

The Johnston County, N. C., road shown at the *left* was no longer a local joke. It was felt to be an unnecessary nuisance which hindered the development of the region.

Courtesy, North Carolina State Department of Archives and History, Raleigh

At least an oil-dressing could be applied to bind the surface and keep dust down. (*Right*).

Courtesy, Public Roads Administration, Washington, D. C.

Some towns and cities were laying down full concrete roads and sidewalks in 1908.

Courtesy, Public Roads Administration, Washington, D. C.

Oil

As the coming of the motor age increased the demand for petroleum products, new fields were located and drilled; new methods of processing crude oil were developed.

At the *right* is a newly developed well near El Campo, Tex., as it looked in 1908.

Courtesy, The Library of the University of Texas, Austin

At the *left* is a 1910 gusher at Lakeview, Okla. A few hours after this picture was taken, the derrick was blown away.

Photo by United States Geological Survey
Courtesy, Scribner Art File

In many small communities, the "kerosene" wagon continued to call with oil for lamps and stoves. The picture *right* was taken in 1909 at Hempstead, N. Y.

Courtesy, The Hempstead Library, Hempstead, N. Y.

Air News: 1909-1910

Popular Mechanics, June, 1909. *Courtesy*, Popular Mechanics, Chicago, Ill.

Airplane design was still fluid. The contraption at the *left* was being offered the Army for military use.

At the *right* is an unusual picture of the Wright Brothers in 1910. Orville wears the moustache.

Courtesy, Scribner Art File

Glenn Curtiss was at the controls of the craft shown *left* as an Army officer tested flight marksmanship with a rifle.

Town & Country, Sept. 10, 1910. *Courtesy*, Town & Country, New York City

In Panama

The great ditch across the Isthmus was being pushed on towards completion. Col. Goethals, chief engineer, and Dr. Gorgas, sanitary chief, had had their differences but each had done his indispensable work and the end was in sight. *Below* is shown the site of Gatun Dam as it looked in 1909.

Courtesy, The National Archives, Washington, D. C.

A year later, this picture of the eastern lock of Gatun Dam was made; a testimony of remarkable progress.

Harper's Weekly, Aug. 13, 1910. *Courtesy,* Harper & Brothers, New York City

Presidential Embarrassment

President Taft was finding the going rather rough. He had been edged and nagged into actions which roused against him the progressive elements of his own party.

Harper's Weekly, May 7, 1910. *Courtesy,* Harper & Brothers, New York City

When he opened the 1910 baseball season at Washington (as shown *left*), the effect of the democratic gesture was lost on the public. The popular hero he had succeeded was back in the picture.

Harper's Weekly, June 25, 1910
Courtesy, Harper & Brothers, New York City

Theodore Roosevelt, fresh from a European tour on which he had received unprecedented honors and attention, is seen at the *right* as he greeted cheering New York crowds in June, 1910.

"T. R." lost no time rebuilding his political fences. He is shown *below* greeting his Rough Riders at Central Park Plaza.

Harper's Weekly, June 25, 1910. *Courtesy,* Harper & Brothers, New York City

9
THE ENGINES OF CHANGE

By 1911, social and political reformers were publicizing their respective blueprints for the celestial city with all the resources of contemporary advertising. They had learned the value of "pressure" applied to the recalcitrant.

Supporters of suffrage for women claimed that politics would be purged of sin, once the ladies had a vote. The picture at the *right* shows part of the great demonstration of suffragettes on Fifth Avenue, New York, in May, 1911.

Harper's Weekly, May 20, 1911
Courtesy, Harper & Brothers, New York City

Headed by a band of pipers, the parade featured tableaux like the one shown *above,* wherein were pictured woman's estate and influence down through the centuries.

Less spectacular but just as hard-hitting, the anti-liquor drive of the Women's Christian Temperance Union rolled towards its objective. At the *right,* Mrs. Lillian Stevens, the Union's President, is seen at a Maine rally in September, 1911.

Harper's Weekly, Oct. 7, 1911. *Courtesy,* Harper & Brothers, New York City

Child Labor

Aggressive action to prevent employment of minors in mills and factories began as the public was made to realize the vast number of children so employed. The pictures *below* were given wide distribution around 1912 in support of reform.

The boy shown *above* worked a sixty-hour week in a Virginia glass factory.

The wage for child oyster-shuckers in the Louisiana cannery shown *below* was ten cents a day.

Both illustrations on this page are from the Jacob A. Riis Collection. *Courtesy*, Museum of the City of New York

Hookworm

Favorable climatic conditions had made the Southeastern states a focus for hookworm—a parasite whose infection reduced industrious, intelligent people to mere shiftless automata. Dr. C. W. Stiles enlisted the aid of the Rockefellers in studying the disease and effectively controlling it.

In the picture *above*, Dr. Stiles is seen in the center by the tent post as he supervises a field clinic at Jacksonville, N. C.

To county dispensaries like the one in Lincoln County, N. C., shown *below*, people from every part of the back country flocked for a diagnosis and treatment.

The Role of Science

As nature continued to reveal her secrets to American scientists and engineers, the public began to look up to such men just as earlier generations had reverenced powerful preachers and astute statesmen. Science was going to make the better world possible.

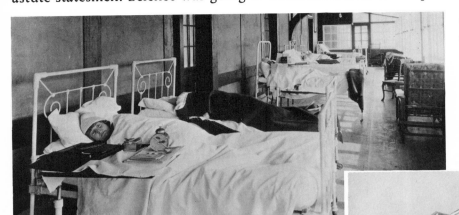

Courtesy, Stony Wold Sanatorium, New York City

The "white plague" — tuberculosis — was successfully fought in new ways. Open-air treatment in the Adirondack Mountains of New York State is shown at the *left.*

The first Gyro-Compass (*right*) was installed aboard the *U.S.S. Delaware* in 1911. This navigational necessity operated free of stray magnetic disturbances.

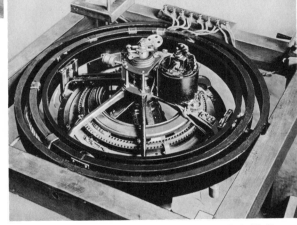

Courtesy, Sperry Gyroscope Company, Inc., Great Neck, N. Y.

Curtiss's 1911 flying-boat *below* was the prototype of modern seaplanes.

Courtesy, Scribner Art File

Scientific Hobbies

Children played with miniature steel beams and construction parts; with mechanical railroads and chemistry "sets." One of the newest electrical arts, that of radio, was given notable impetus by the experiments of amateur or "ham" operators.

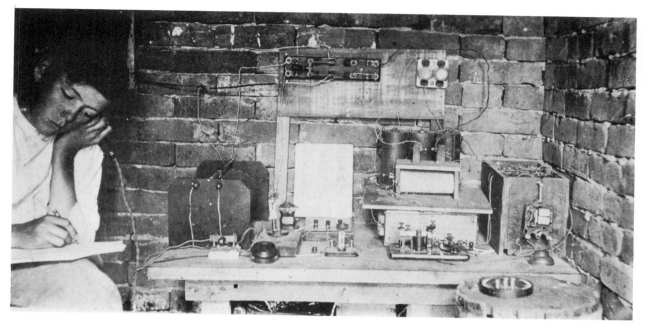

The homemade "rig" shown *above* was typical of thousands of cellar "wireless" stations in 1911.

The amateur station shown *below* could match many professional installations. Note the De Forest audion detector just right of center.

Both illustrations on this page are by the *courtesy* of The American Radio Relay League, West Hartford, Conn.

Copper

Copper production rose as electric power, light and heat were more extensively applied in industry and the home.

The miners at the *left* were drilling deep under the Montana soil, preparatory to blasting.

Back east in New Jersey, the refined metal was produced by an electrolytic process. The picture *below* shows the cathodes lifted from the solution.

Both illustrations on this page are by the *courtesy* of The Anaconda Company, New York City

Shipbuilding

Courtesy, American Car and Foundry Company, New York City

The slow death of what had been a great American industry continued without much hope of revival. So long as American merchants gave their business to foreign ships, shipyards like the one in Wilmington, Del., shown *above* did the best they could with scows and coasting vessels. The thriving commerce on the Great Lakes, however, produced a demand for home-built carriers like the grain ship shown *below*, loading at Duluth, Minn.

Courtesy, St. Louis County Historical Society, Duluth, Minn.

Finance

Alarmed by popular clamor against capital, Wall Street men insisted that the primary job of "the Street" was the financing of new business and not the encouragement of speculation. The floor of the New York Stock Exchange is seen at the *left* as it looked in 1911.

Harper's Weekly, Nov. 18, 1911
Courtesy, Harper & Brothers, New York City

Anti-Trust

Legendary figures of American finance were now anxious and ready to justify their operations to the public. At the *right*, John D. Rockefeller is testifying in one of the anti-trust actions brought against his oil companies.

Courtesy, Underwood-Stratton, New York City

Labor Trouble

The trial of the McNamara brothers (shown *left* with Samuel Gompers) for the bombing of the anti-union Los Angeles *Times* was a sensation of 1911. The unexpected "guilty" pleas entered by the men gave a severe shock to the forces of labor which had organized to defend them.

Courtesy, Underwood-Stratton, New York City

The "Curb" in 1912

At Broad Street and Exchange Place, New York City, where of old the merchants of New Amsterdam met for trading, members of the Curb Exchange dealt in securities which the conservative Stock Exchange declined to list. Many of the newer industries were financed on the Curb. In rain, in blizzards or under the burning sun the members had only the middle of the street.

In the window "offices" shown *above*, the clerks of the Curb brokers watched for signals of transactions from the traders in the street *below*.

Both illustrations on this page are by the *courtesy* of The American Stock Exchange, New York City

Education on the March

Leaders in education felt that they, rather than the men of science or the men of money, could ensure the golden age to come. The teacher became the "educator," much as the undertaker became the "mortician."

The old disciplines of learning were replaced by the "motivated" lesson. In the picture at the *left*, the children are learning to read and spell by printing labels for their toys.

Prospective teachers of the class of 1914 at a Pennsylvania normal school are being taught to play in the picture at the *right*.

Less time was devoted to study and more to development of the child's physical equipment. At the *left*, Chicago school children are enjoying an afternoon in a public swimming pool.

All illustrations on this page are from Louis W. Rapeer, *Teaching Elementary School Subjects.* 1917

The Colleges

The fervor of change and uplift which worked in educators on the elementary and secondary levels was not experienced by their brethren in the colleges, nor was it required of them.

The undergraduate of 1911 gloried in elemental sport like the "class rush" shown *above*. When he occupied the typical room shown *below*, his thoughts did not as a rule dwell on the faults of the curriculum. He kept his distance from the Faculty and expected it to reciprocate.

Both illustrations on this page are by the *courtesy* of Princeton University Library and R. C. Rose & Son, Princeton, N. J.

The Colleges (*Continued*)

The practical sex, however, took a more serious view of college. The Purdue girls of the class of 1914 at the *left* were preparing for scientific careers or for matrimony.

Over tea and homemade chocolate cake they relaxed on occasions like the dormitory party shown *right*.

Not the least important activity of any young woman at college was "dating." In the picture at the *left*, the girls in the background were not being particularly helpful.

All illustrations on this page are by the *courtesy* of Purdue University, Lafayette, Ind.

Extremes in Art

Through 1911 and 1912, John Sloan continued to produce moody *genre* studies of New York life like "Six O'Clock" at the *right* and "McSorley's Bar" *below*.

Courtesy, Phillips Memorial Gallery, Washington, D. C.

Courtesy, Detroit Institute of Arts, Mich.

But the layman "who knew what he liked" was more pleased with a painting by Paul Chabas — the study of "September Morn" at the *right*, whose popularity was immediate in 1912 — and thereafter.

International Studio, August, 1912

Motors and Movies

The change in American standards of sexual behavior, brought about by the dark anonymity provided in movie theaters and by the freedom of environment which the automobile afforded, belongs to a later date.

Courtesy, Mrs. Frank Ewing, Grand Rapids, Mich.

In 1912, when this Grant, Mich., family went for a ride, father drove the car. It was his hobby; and it stayed home nights.

Electric broughams were recommended for ladies because "the most delicate frame would not be jolted and the slow, comfortable pace allowed a leisurely study of the scenery."

In the picture *right*, Annette Kellermann is seen getting into a Rauch and Lang electric.

Town & Country, Jan. 6, 1912.
Courtesy, Town & Country, New York City

Town & Country, June 22, 1912. Courtesy, Town & Country, New York City

In 1912 some Eastern summer resorts still banned the use of automobiles, but, as the picture at the *left* indicates, a progressive Los Angeles country club took the opposite tack.

Motors and Movies (*Continued*)

The motion picture, regardless of the precincts where it might be shown, was coming of age as mature entertainment. The still picture *above* is a scene from "Queen Elizabeth," starring Sarah Bernhardt and Lou Tellegen. This French import, shown here in 1912, was the first "feature" picture and had great influence on the domestic product.

Mary Pickford and Lionel Barrymore appear in the still *below*, a scene from D. W. Griffith's 1912 picture "The New York Hat."

Both illustrations on this page are by the *courtesy* of the Film Library, The Museum of Modern Art, New York City

Frontier Turns Inward

James J. Hill stepped forward proudly to address the crowd on completion of his Great Northern line to Bend, Ore. (*left*), but in 1911 the empire-builder was already an anachronism. The pioneer days were done. The popular mind dwelt less on producing great works and scheming great schemes than on diverting to reform and reconstruction the energies that had peopled the wilderness.

No lands were left which had about them the mystery and hopefulness which could draw men and women in search of fortune across half a continent. On the Montana homestead *below*, there was only the prospect of a hard and lonely struggle for bread.

Both illustrations on this page are by the *courtesy* of the Great Northern Railway Company, St. Paul, Minn.

Sport

Correct management of the reins and position of the hands were stressed in recommending to 1912 ladies the smartness of a four-in-hand turnout. (*Right*).

Belle Beach, *Riding and Driving for Women.* 1912

Belle Beach, *Riding and Driving for Women.* 1912

The costume at the *left* was considered *chic* for young horsewomen when they rode astride.

Below is a group of winter sportsfolk setting off across the New Hampshire hills. Popular magazines of 1912 commented on the growing vogue of winter sports and winter holidays.

Town & Country, Jan. 13, 1912. *Courtesy,* Town & Country, New York City

Girls

The little Chicago girl at the *left* included her family in the picture. Note the ornate style of beauty featured in dolls of the period.

The photograph of a Chicago girls' club at *right* was also taken around 1911.

Both illustrations on this page are *courtesy* of the Chicago Lawn Historical Society and Chicago Public Library, Illinois.

Courtesy, Mr. Myron F. Henkel, Springfield, Illinois

Sport clothes for girls were not yet fully
functional, as the 1912 picture *above* indicates.

Militia

Units which offered full-dress outfits, like those of the Maryland regiment pictured *below* in
1911, had no trouble filling their companies.

Courtesy, The Peale Museum, Baltimore, Md.

Turned Out to Graze

The end of the road for many fire-horses came in 1911. Most of the larger cities motorized their departments or planned to do so.

Harper's Weekly, Apr. 1, 1911. *Courtesy*, Harper & Brothers, New York City

New York City put "high-pressure" hose trucks (*left*) in service.

The Mack motor-pumper shown *below* was the 1911 model. At the *right* is a 1912 chemical truck by American-La France.

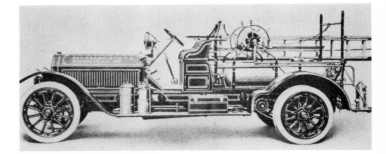

Courtesy, Mack-International Motor Truck Corporation, New York City

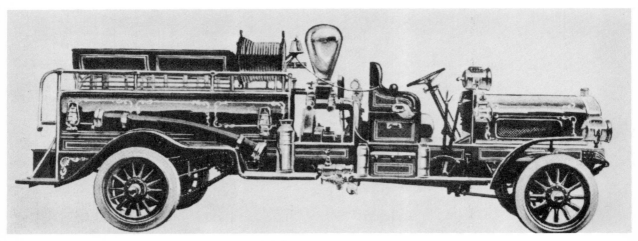

Courtesy, Mack-International Motor Truck Corporation, New York City

The City as Symbol

The nation's ambitious youth thronged to the restless and opulent cities. This was no longer a natural process whereby those who were unprovided for in smaller communities were forced to adventure. In these years of change, the cities symbolized a larger and freer way of life—the rich peace of the future for which man would not have to strive.

Renascent San Francisco's Market Street is seen *right* as it looked in 1911.

Harper's Weekly, Màr. 2, 1912. *Courtesy*, Harper & Brothers, New York City

Richmond, Va., as a true city of the newly-industrial South, bragged of its "skyline." Contrast the 1912 view *below* with the picture on page 29.

Courtesy, The Valentine Museum, Richmond, Va.

In the News: 1912

Early in the year, striking textile workmen at Lawrence, Mass., carried flags up against the bayonets of the militiamen who protected strikebreakers at work. But the presence of I. W. W. organizers lost the strikers popular support.

Below, President Taft is seen signing the proclamation that made Arizona the forty-eighth state—on St. Valentine's Day.

Harper's Weekly, Feb. 10, 1912
Courtesy, Harper & Brothers, New York City

Harper's Weekly, Mar. 2, 1912
Courtesy, Harper & Brothers, New York City

New dance steps were improvised to suit at once the ragtime music newly come up from the honky-tonks and barrel-houses, and the hobble skirts which were the vogue. At the *left*, a couple are pictured in one of the positions of the "Turkey Trot."

Courtesy, Brown Brothers, New York City

Titanic

Early in April, 1912, the unsinkable luxury liner *Titanic* sailed from Liverpool on her maiden voyage. She is seen at the *right* in her last photograph.

Four hundred miles southeast of Cape Race, she struck an iceberg at twenty-one knots. Her hull was slit open from bow to stern. Three hours later she went down.

At the New York pier, the crowds shown *left* waited anxiously for news, and for the rescue ship *Carpathia* which had arrived at the scene some hours after the disaster.

As the *Carpathia* was worked up to the pier (*right*), her boats still hung from the davits. But of *Titanic's* 2,223 souls, only 705 had been rescued.

All illustrations on this page are by the *courtesy* of Brown Brothers, New York City

Gunmen

For more than two years the newspapers featured the repercussions of the Rosenthal murder. On July 15, 1912, Rosenthal, a gambling-house proprietor in New York City, appeared before District Attorney Charles S. Whitman and swore that Police Lieutenant Charles Becker (*left*) was his partner and cover-up man. A few hours later, four gunmen shot Rosenthal dead in front of the Metropole Hotel on 43rd Street near Broadway. Becker was convicted as an accessory to the murder and was executed after several futile appeals.

The "gunmen," a new type in American crime, were also convicted and executed. They are seen *below* on their way to Sing Sing Prison in November, 1912. Reading right to left, obliquely back, starting with the man holding the cigarette: Lefty Louie, Dago Frank, Gyp the Blood, Whitey Lewis.

Both illustrations on this page are by the *courtesy* of Brown Brothers, New York City

Three Way Election

The Republican Party approached convention time in a hopeless fight over the interparty issue of "progressivism" versus "stand-pattism"—reform or reaction. Theodore Roosevelt had determined to block renomination of his erstwhile. friend, President Taft.

Progressive Republicans favored Senator Robert LaFollette of Wisconsin (at *right*, with Taft). It was generally believed that Roosevelt would not run. But in February, 1912, he changed his mind and entered the battle against the "stand-pat" bosses of his party. "We stand at Armageddon and we battle for the Lord," said he, but the convention bosses at Chicago (*below*) held the line for Taft.

Courtesy, Culver Pictures, Inc., New York City

Harper's Weekly, June 29, 1912
Courtesy, Harper & Brothers, New York City

In August, 1912, at another Chicago convention pictured *right*, the outraged and "steamrollered" Progressive Republicans formed a new party and chose Theodore Roosevelt as its nominee.

Courtesy, Brown Brothers, New York City

Three Way Election (*Continued*)

"Strong as a Bull Moose" was a favorite simile of the Progressive candidate, and the figure of that animal joined the donkey and the elephant as a party symbol.

Courtesy, Brown Brothers, New York City

When news of his nomination was brought to T.R. at his Long Island home, he responded with the characteristic smile shown at the *left*. *Below* is the Bull Moose emblem as used on a 1912 campaign badge.

Courtesy, Roosevelt Memorial Association, New York City

The "New Freedom"

The Democrats at their Baltimore convention had found an exciting candidate. The crusading Governor of New Jersey, and former President of Princeton University, backed by Bryan and a re-invigorated party, revealed great campaigning gifts. Woodrow Wilson struck hard at the forces of privilege in addresses like the one pictured *below*, made before an Iowa college group.

Harper's Weekly, Sept. 28, 1912. *Courtesy*, Harper & Brothers, New York City

Scholar in Politics

Taft's chances had been effectually killed by Roosevelt's pre-convention sneers and accusations. But in Wilson, the Democrats had a candidate who out-Roosevelted Roosevelt. People listened to him and believed him, as he carried his gospel of the "New Freedom" to great meeting halls and to little corner groups like the Minnesota people shown *below*.

Poised and serene, Wilson with his gift for phrases, painted bright word-pictures of a better world. He gave a vision to the man in the street. He was confident of victory as he cast his vote in a Princeton, N. J., fire house on Nov. 5, 1912.

Both illustrations on this page are by the *courtesy* of Underwood-Stratton, New York City

10

THE NEW FREEDOM

Woodrow Wilson triumphed over a divided Republican Party in 1912. The electoral vote ran 435 for Wilson; 88 for Roosevelt and the Progressives; 8 for Taft.

Harper's Weekly, Nov. 9, 1912
Courtesy, Harper & Brothers, New York City

The aims of the new administration were synthesized in the phrase, "The New Freedom," originally the title given the new President's public statements when they appeared in book form, and by 1913 accepted as a slogan for political action against monopolies and greed. In many minds the new freedom extended far beyond political and economic ends, and foreshadowed an American Utopia for body and spirit.

Left, Woodrow Wilson, twenty-seventh person to be President of the United States.

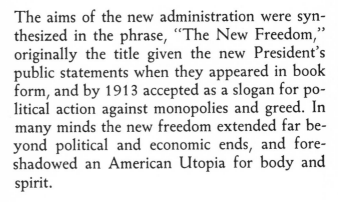

Courtesy, Underwood-Stratton, New York City

Ex-President Taft wore a pleased smile as he rode to the inauguration with President Wilson, as shown *right*.

"This is not a day of triumph; it is a day of dedication," said the new President, "we shall restore, not destroy."

Courtesy, Brown Brothers, New York City

At the *left* is the first official photograph of the new Cabinet. Prominent in the right foreground is William Jennings Bryan, the Secretary of State.

Stand and Deliver

Weary of the fight to secure local approval of votes for women by action of the State Legislatures, a newly "militant" wing of the Suffragettes heckled the Wilson administration for woman's share in the new freedom.

In 1913, the militant forces of suffrage paraded through the streets of Washington, D. C., and demanded an amendment to the Federal Constitution which would blanket all local opposition to their cause.

Both illustrations on this page are by the *courtesy* of the Scribner Art File

Postal Progress

On Jan. 1, 1913, the new Parcel Post service had begun to operate. The farmer in isolated locations was now able to buy in markets where his dollar went farther, and he was given an opportunity of closer contact with his fellow citizens by a generally improving rural post system.

The picture at the *left* was taken at a Washington, D. C. post office on the first day of Parcel Post service. Now, packages would be taken by Uncle Sam to places which the express companies could not serve.

Harper's Weekly, Jan. 18, 1913. *Courtesy*, Harper & Brothers, New York City

At the *right*, the RFD man crosses a ford in Lauderdale County, Ala., c. 1913.

Courtesy, Public Roads Administration, Washington, D. C.

The close-up picture of a rural mail wagon at the *left* was taken in 1913 near Greenwood, Miss.

Courtesy, Public Roads Administration, Washington, D. C.

News From Panama

American engineers were beating the world again. The work on the great Isthmian Canal was almost completed.

Courtesy, The National Archives, Washington, D. C.

The picture of Gatun Locks *above* was taken on June 25, 1913. In the distance is the Atlantic entrance to the Canal. *Below* are shown the lower main gates of Miroflores Locks as they looked on July 5, 1913.

Courtesy, Scribner Art File

End of a Great Task

In Culebra Cut (*above*) and other ways through the mountains, the work was impeded by "slides" or cave-ins of the walls. Note a recent slide at the right, *above*.

Despite all difficulties, on Sept. 9, 1913, steamshovels Number 226 and 204 took the last bites from the bottom of the Panama Canal. The historic moment is shown in the picture *below*.

Both illustrations on this page are by the *courtesy* of the Scribner Art File

Movie "Stars"

The motion picture in its infancy was encountering an evil with which the stage had long been plagued. American theater-goers went to see, not plays or stories, but personalities.

D. W. Griffith directed "Judith of Bethulia," but it is safe to say that it was a 1913 hit because it "featured" Blanche Sweet (shown *right* in a scene from the picture) and Mae Marsh (*below*, with Robert Harron).

Little boys paid out their dimes to see William S. Hart (at the extreme *right*); the vehicle in which he appeared meant little or nothing.

South of the Border

Backwash from Mexico's internal troubles had been spilling over Uncle Sam's doorstep ever since 1911. Early in 1914, President Wilson demanded formal apologies for the arrest of some United States marines at Tampico, Mexico. When President Huerta of Mexico refused the demand, President Wilson ordered the Atlantic fleet to Vera Cruz.

Courtesy, Scribner Art File

On Apr. 21, 1914, the city of Vera Cruz was taken with slight loss to the marines and sailors who made the landing.

There was comparatively little reaction. The average native of Vera Cruz docilely accepted another set of rulers and rules.

The American passion for sanitation was loosed on the captured city. At the *left*, United States sailors are supervising an apathetic job of street sweeping.

Courtesy, Scribner Art File

Colorado Strike

From September, 1913, until May, 1914, south-central Colorado was in a state of civil war. Long-standing differences between the Colorado Fuel and Iron Company and its miners resulted in a strike of singular bitterness, which was not settled until Federal troops restored order and the company adopted a more constructive policy.

Courtesy, Harper's Weekly, May 23, 1914

The picture of strikers *above* was taken near a tent city they had set up in the vicinity of San Rafael, Colo.

Below, a mine guard is shown behind a breastwork. This picture was taken shortly after a shocking encounter at Ludlow, Colo., in April, 1914, during which many innocent persons were killed. The breastwork was made of ruins from the Ludlow fire.

Telephone

On June 17, 1914, the last pole was set for the first transcontinental telephone line—a direct wire, New York to San Francisco. The picture at the *left* was taken on the spot. The line was opened for service in January, 1915.

Expansion of telephone service was playing its part in bringing all Americans closer together. The rural mails and parcel post, and now the telephone, were breaking down the lonesomeness of people far from the cities—"the lones" as pioneer women called it. The man in the picture *right* might have been making a business call, or he might have been minding the neighbors' business on a "party line."

Both illustrations on this page are by the *courtesy* of the American Telephone and Telegraph Company, New York City

A War

The murder of the Austrian Archduke Franz Ferdinand and his wife, late in June, 1914, had created a new European crisis, but most Americans had become accustomed to European "crises" since 1911. Our own troubles with Mexico seemed much more important. And so the headlines *below* had for the general public the quality of nightmare.

On July 29, 1914, the war news ran across only five columns. The weather report read "Fair Today and Tomorrow." Mme. Caillaux had been acquitted. Two New Yorkers had attempted suicide.

By August 2, the headlines spread across the entire page as "the lights of Europe were going out."

By August 4, a general European war was in being.

All illustrations on this page are by the *courtesy* of the New York *Herald-Tribune*, New York City

Reaction

Courtesy, Underwood-Stratton, New York City

"All German hearts beat higher," said one of the German language newspapers published in New York, and in that city reservists of the German army paraded as seen *above*, carrying their national flag. Some of these men sailed to rejoin their regiments.

The Canal Opened

S. S. Ancon is shown *below* as she passed Cucaracha Slide on Aug. 15, 1914—the day on which the Panama Canal was opened for traffic. As they read their newspapers, military men recalled *U. S. S. Oregon's* voyage around Cape Horn in 1898, and felt that Uncle Sam's new tactical ditch had been finished none too soon.

Courtesy, National Archives, Washington, D. C.

Highways

All through 1914, work continued on the good roads program. The nation's road system was becoming a really efficient network for general transport, for pleasure driving, or for possible emergencies.

In many sections, excavating was done by hand as seen in the 1914 picture at the *right*.

Courtesy, Public Roads Administration, Washington, D. C.

Courtesy, North Carolina State Department of Archives and History, Raleigh

Keeping the roads in good repair was an essential part of the program. At the *left*, men of New Hanover County, N. C., are patching their section of a State Highway.

First proposed in 1912, the Lincoln Highway began to be built in October, 1914. This coast-to-coast link for motorists between New York and San Francisco was financed in its early days by private contributions and State grants. At the *right*, a touring car heads across a Wyoming stretch of the road in 1914.

Town & Country, Jan. 3, 1914. *Courtesy*, Town & Country, New York City

Stores and Offices

The architecture of business offices and retail stores remained stubbornly conservative in conception. The advertising or "public relations" value of a cleverly designed place of business was not widely appreciated.

Courtesy, The Great Atlantic and Pacific Tea Company, New York City

In the view of a chain store *above*, note how much "brand name" canned goods was stocked by 1914, in addition to teas, coffees and dairy products.

The office pictured *below* was in the old County Building at Carson City, Nev.

Courtesy, Nevada State Historical Society, Reno

Funny Folk

The movies in 1914 abounded in comedy of the slap-stick school. Several of the comedians became famous in their day for their performances as distinctive, national types.

The fun in a fat man's troubles was ably exploited by John Bunny (*above*, in a tense moment from "Father's Flirtation").

Flora Finch (*below*, in striped dress) was the perennial lean and hungry spinster. A 1914 comedy entitled "The New Stenographer" provided the scene *below*.

Both illustrations on this page are by the *courtesy* of Photoplay, New York City

"New Freedom" in Literature

Critics were being forced to recognize clamorous new voices in the national literary chorus. The young writers of the Middle West somewhat aggressively declared their artistic independence of Boston and New York.

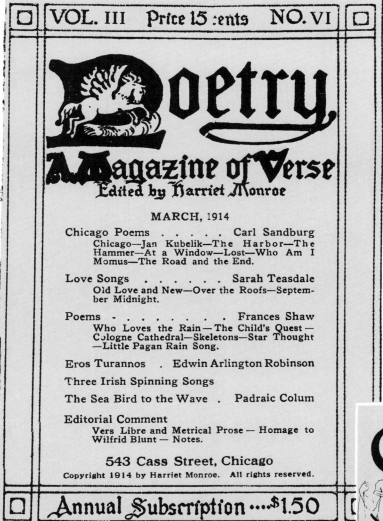

VOL. III   Price 15 cents   NO. VI

Poetry
A Magazine of Verse
Edited by Harriet Monroe

MARCH, 1914

Chicago Poems . . . . . Carl Sandburg
    Chicago—Jan Kubelik—The Harbor—The
    Hammer—At a Window—Lost—Who Am I
    Momus—The Road and the End.

Love Songs . . . . . Sarah Teasdale
    Old Love and New—Over the Roofs—Septem-
    ber Midnight.

Poems - . . . . Frances Shaw
    Who Loves the Rain—The Child's Quest—
    Cologne Cathedral—Skeletons—Star Thought
    —Little Pagan Rain Song.

Eros Turannos . Edwin Arlington Robinson

Three Irish Spinning Songs

The Sea Bird to the Wave . Padraic Colum

Editorial Comment
    Vers Libre and Metrical Prose — Homage to
    Wilfrid Blunt — Notes.

543 Cass Street, Chicago
Copyright 1914 by Harriet Monroe. All rights reserved.

Annual Subscription ····$1.50

Poetry: A Magazine of Verse, March, 1914
Courtesy, Poetry, Chicago, Ill.

In the issue of *Poetry: A Magazine of Verse* shown at the *left,* the new spirit is aptly illustrated by Carl Sandburg's "Chicago Poems" and by the editorial on the then-burning question of "free verse."

Far forward in the attack on the genteel tradition was a New York magazine, *The Smart Set,* which published many of the new writers and strove determinedly to be ahead of the intellectual fashion. Note, on the cover reproduced *right,* the motto at the lower left.

The Smart Set, October, 1914

New Art From Abroad

Courtesy, Mr. & Mrs. Walter C. Arensberg, Hollywood, Calif.

Marcel Duchamp's "Nude Descending a Staircase" *above* was the principal target for popular wit during the Armory Show, but the crowd had a good laugh at Cezanne and Van Gogh as well.

Sad to say, the announcement of another visiting artist (at the *right* in all its austerity of phrase) met with much more popular approval.

Work which was believed to exemplify the modern spirit in art was arranged for display in the Armory of the Sixty-ninth Regiment, New York City, during February, 1913. Cubism and Post-Impressionism were revealed to the public at this remarkable exhibition of painting and sculpture.

Town & Country, Feb. 1, 1915
Courtesy, Town & Country, New York City

Campus By Day

The American collegian remained still pretty much of a sartorial conformist.

Courtesy, Purdue University, Lafayette, Ind.

A cheerful, and sometimes irritating, breeziness of manner went with the clothes shown *above*, as worn by a group at Purdue University in 1913.

Smith College girls did their gymnasium work in 1913 with notable snap and vigor, as may be observed in the piece of documentation given *below*.

Courtesy, Smith College Archives, Northampton, Mass.

In the Evening by the Moonlight

But Young America at college aimed at a suave cosmopolitanism when attending the "Proms" of those years.

Courtesy, Smith College Archives, Northampton, Mass.

A group of Smith College girls (Class of 1915) are shown *above* with their escorts, *en route* to their own Prom in 1914.

Dancers

The personal charm and flawless taste of Vernon and Irene Castle won the nation away by sheer force of example from the wilder manifestations of the new ragtime. To the romantic youth of 1915, they were what the Gibson Man and the Gibson Girl had been to a previous generation.

At the *left*, they are seen in a step of the tango; *below*, in a ballroom dance pose.

Both illustrations on this page are by the *courtesy* of Mrs. Irene Castle Enzinger, Lake Forest, Ill.

May 1, 1915

For many months, pictures and text in the nation's press kept the American public at the ringside of the war in Europe. The Central Powers had the sympathy of many; equally strong sympathies were aroused for France and England. The majority of Americans were neutral, and somewhat puzzled as diplomatic "notes" were directed to both sides protesting interference with our shipping.

Courtesy, Scribner Art File

The Cunard liner *Lusitania* (*left*) was to sail for Liverpool from New York on the morning of Saturday, May 1, 1915. She was unarmed and carried only small-arms ammunition in her cargo. This was in accord with United States law.

On the morning of the sailing, among resort announcements from Atlantic City and the Adirondacks, New York newspapers carried the two advertisements shown in conjunction at the extreme *right*.

Courtesy, The Sun, New York City

One hundred and twenty-eight American citizens were lost in the event described *above*, a blunder that turned American opinion sharply against Germany and her allies.

Disaster at Chicago

The mind of the Middle West, however, was more strongly moved to pity and terror by the capsizing of the excursion steamer *Eastland* at her pier in the Chicago River on July 24, 1915, as she was preparing to leave for a day's outing on Lake Michigan. More than eight hundred of the two thousand persons aboard lost their lives.

Courtesy, Brown Brothers, New York City

Above, the *Eastland* is shown lying on her side after the disaster.

Houston

In August, 1915, the *S. S. Satilla* (in the foreground *below*) brought a cargo of freight up the new ship channel at Houston, Tex., and had the honor of opening Houston's wharves to deep-water traffic.

Courtesy, Houston Chamber of Commerce, Tex.

Panama-Pacific Exposition

Between February and December, 1915, the opening of the Panama Canal and the discovery of the Pacific Ocean were celebrated jointly in a great Exposition at San Francisco, Calif. The use of Californian architectural styles in the buildings at the Exposition (*below*, the Home Economy and Commerce Buildings) brought about a national vogue for Spanish houses and decoration.

Courtesy, Scribner Art File

The Canal as a Weapon

Although "slides" or cave-ins were still making trouble, the importance of the Panama Canal to national defense was undoubted. In the picture *below*, taken on Aug. 31, 1915, *U.S.S. Ohio* (at *left*) and *U.S.S. Missouri* are seen passing through the upper chamber of Miraflores Locks.

Courtesy, National Archives, Washington, D. C.

Propaganda

As the warring groups competed for the support of United States public opinion, our newspapers were filled with charges and countercharges of atrocious conduct, plus fervent declarations of national virtue. In August, 1915, headlines like those shown *below* awoke the American public to some evil connotations of propaganda.

Yet the pictures of ruined cathedrals and the vivid stories sent back early in the war by correspondents like the veteran Richard Harding Davis (*below*) were propaganda also.

HOW GERMANY HAS WORKED IN U. S. TO SHAPE OPINION, BLOCK THE ALLIES AND GET MUNITIONS FOR HERSELF, TOLD IN SECRET AGENTS' LETTERS.

LETTERS MR. VIERECK AND DR. ALBERT WROTE TO EACH OTHER.

Chancellor, Ambassador, Financial Agent and Bankers Chief Figures in Vast Scheme Revealed in Documents Obtained by The World—Fatherland Financed, Author Fox's Expenses Paid, Plans Laid to Buy Press Association and Otherwise Control News of the War.

German heavy-handedness in the execution of a program of intrigue and conspiracy climaxed in the revelations headlined at the top of the page. These were the result of the loss of a briefcase by Dr. Heinrich Albert, chief of German espionage in the United States. In consequence, the German military attache, Franz von Papen (*right*), and other diplomats were shipped back to Germany.

All illustrations on this page are by the *courtesy* of the Scribner Art File

War Boom

After a brief, shocked slump in 1914 at the declaration of the European war, American industry entered on an almost feverish period of activity. Foreign orders came piling in as the belligerents cast their manpower into battle.

Southern mills like the one on Tar River, N. C., at the *left* were in full production and bringing hard money to a section which could use it.

Courtesy, North Carolina State Department of Archives and History, Raleigh

War needs gave the builders of internal combustion engines a chance for vast expansion. At the *right* is the plant of the Waukesha Motor Co. in southeastern Wisconsin as it looked in 1915.

Courtesy, Waukesha County Historical Society, Waukesha, Wis.

In New Orleans, La., the public grain elevator at the *left* was completed in 1916, and was part of a program for improving shipping facilities at that port.

Courtesy, Board of Commissioners of the Port of New Orleans, La.

Machinery

Many pieces of machinery familiar to a later generation were in an experimental stage between 1913 and 1916.

At the *right* a 1913 model of a Diesel power unit is shown.

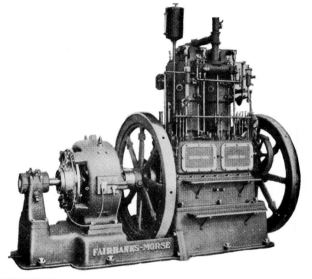

Courtesy, Fairbanks, Morse & Co., Chicago, Ill.

Courtesy, International Harvester Company, Chicago, Ill.

The kerosene tractor at the *left* was designed in 1915 for use on small farms.

The biplane at the *right*, designed and produced in 1916, was Boeing Aircraft Company's first model.

Courtesy, Boeing Aircraft Company, Seattle, Wash.

Music and Words

Courtesy, Hardman, Peck & Co., New York City

Mechanization of our society reached a climax in the "player-piano" or "Pianola," a once-familiar object in aspiring parlors. A 1916 "player" is shown *left*. Note the perforated roll which rendered Chopin and Schubert with soul-shattering precision.

In 1916, the all-purpose "audion," shown with its adapter at the *right*, was on sale for experimental use as detector, amplifier, or oscillator.

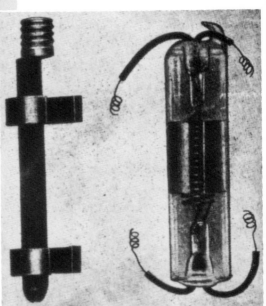

The Electrical Experimenter, May, 1916
Courtesy, Popular Mechanics, Chicago, Ill.

Courtesy, Dictaphone Corporation, New York City

The 1915 Dictaphone at the *left* was finding favor with a newly-christened American type—the "executive," whose brilliant ideas could brook no delay in expression.

Iron

The two nations which up to 1914 led the United States in steel and iron exports were now at war with each other. The market was wide open.

The Fayal Mine at Eveleth, Minn., was one of many American mines which profited by the situation. The open pit of the Fayal Mine is seen in the 1915 picture *above*, and *below* is shown Number Two Station of the works underground.

Both illustrations on this page are by the *courtesy* of the St. Louis County Historical Society, Duluth, Minn.

Steel

Courtesy, Scribner Art File

Through 1915 and 1916 molten pig-iron flowed constantly from the blast furnaces pictured *above*, which, only a year before, were operating at two-thirds capacity.

In the picture *below*, an open-hearth furnace is being tapped. The larger ladle contains the steel; slag pours off into the smaller one.

Courtesy, Bethlehem Steel Company, New York City

Copper

By 1916, the United States was producing sixty-two per cent of the world's supply of copper. Prices were at their peak as munition requirements and other wartime uses demanded more and more of the metal.

Courtesy, The Anaconda Company, New York City

Above is a picture of Butte Hill, Mont., about 1916—the "richest hill on earth."

Dryer and Dryer

A significant number of States had passed prohibitory laws against liquor in the years between 1905 and 1915. The temperance forces, assisted by the refusal of the liquor industry to reform itself, looked forward confidently to the goal of national prohibition.

The old-fashioned saloon (at *left* a specimen at Belle Isle, Richmond, Va.; other specimens on page 193) was the chief target of the crusaders for total prohibition.

Courtesy, The Valentine Museum, Richmond, Va.

Ladies of the Woman's Christian Temperance Union held a jubilant convention at Seattle, Wash., in October, 1915. A partial view of the delegates is given *below*.

Courtesy, National Woman's Christian Temperance Union, Evanston, Ill.

Cigarette Advertising

The cigarette had become by 1914 respectable, virile, accepted. Some public resorts still objected to its use by women; *ladies* did not smoke.

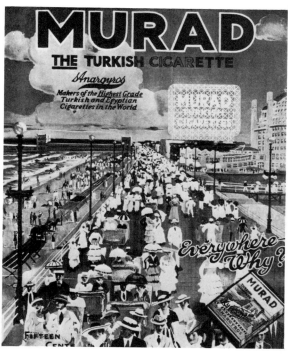

Courtesy, N. W. Ayer & Son, Inc., Philadelphia, Pa.

Courtesy, N. W. Ayer & Son, Inc., Philadelphia, Pa.

Above is the daddy of all popular brands. "Leading medical journals" were said to endorse the purity and wholesomeness of "Sweets."

Note in the advertisement *above*, the appeal to snobbery in the watering-place scene, and the statement that the brand was smoked "Everywhere"—the fashionable everywhere, of course.

The 1915 advertisement at the *right* is a notable specimen of ad-writing. The text repays careful reading for its revelation of the motives on which the advertiser played for response.

Men of Fashion Smoke "Bull" Durham

In the brilliant exodus after a big night at the opera, men who subscribe to boxes for the season—masters of the fine art of enjoyment—utilize the interval before the approach of their limousines in relishing a fresh, delicious smoke of "Bull" Durham tobacco. Theirs are the strong, active hands of self-achievement—capable of controlling the destinies of an industry, or of contriving a perfectly rolled "Bull" Durham cigarette with equal adroitness.

Town & Country, Jan. 1, 1915. Courtesy, Town & Country, New York City

Peace Ship

That the hopes of many men for an international agreement to end the war in Europe might adequately be publicized, Henry Ford was persuaded to charter the neutral liner *Oscar II (below)*. A delegation of peace-loving Americans was to sail aboard her for Norway and Sweden, there to end the conflict by enlisting the mediation of all neutral countries. Unhappily, the effort was a costly if idealistic failure.

Long before the ship sailed on Dec. 4, 1915, the aim of the voyage had been forgotten in the roar of adverse press criticism of the delegates and their boastful public utterances. The statement that "the boys would be out of the trenches by Christmas" and similar promises made the enterprise seem like a colossal joy-ride of fools. Henry Ford is seen at the center *below* (holding hat), with other unidentified delegates.

Both illustrations on this page are *courtesy* of Brown Brothers, New York City

More Movies

The year 1915 saw the making of the first screen "epic," a picture which still has greatness, "The Birth of a Nation." At the *right* is shown a scene from Sherman's march to the sea.

The new medium attracted stars from other firmaments. *Below*, Geraldine Farrar of the Metropolitan Opera is seen in a 1915 movie version of "Carmen," with Wallace Reid.

Courtesy, Film Library, The Museum of Modern Art, New York City

Courtesy, Photoplay, New York City

Football, Etc.

The mysterious sport of curling had its devotees. At the *left*, Nicholas Murray Butler, President of Columbia University, is skipping to the curler in 1915.

Town & Country, Jan. 20, 1915
Courtesy, Town & Country, New York City

Below, the undefeated, untied Pittsburgh team of 1916, called by Walter Camp the best team he had ever seen. "Pop" Warner is on the left end of the second row.

Courtesy, The University of Pittsburgh, Pa.

The New School

The physical plant of American public schools was in process of improvement, along with the curriculum and the faculty.

In sincere praise of the new type of schoolhouse shown at the *right,* a 1915 publication said that it was "as efficient as a modern factory."

L. W. Rapeer, ed., *Educational Hygiene.* 1915

The new type of desk shown *left* was not screwed to the floor. The old rigidity of classroom organization had been owing in great measure to the strictly formal arrangement of classroom furniture. Supervised play, as observed in the Montclair, N. J., picture *below,* was intended to encourage the group spirit.

L. W. Rapeer, *Teaching Elementary School Subjects.* 1917

L. W. Rapeer, *Teaching Elementary School Subjects.* 1917

The Columbus Raid

Continuing forays of Mexican bandits across the border climaxed on the night of Mar. 8, 1916, when about fifteen hundred Mexicans under Pancho Villa raided and looted the town of Columbus, N. M.

The picture *above* was one of the first to be taken after the outrage. The ruins of the town hotel, in which six Americans were killed, may be seen in the *left* foreground.

Six thousand soldiers under command of Brig. Gen. John J. Pershing were ordered to pursue and capture Villa. The General is seen at center foreground *below*, crossing the International Bridge into Mexico.

Both illustrations on this page are *courtesy* of Brown Brothers, New York City

Chasing Villa

Pershing's force advanced some hundreds of miles into Mexico, despite the protests of the Mexican government. Lack of air reconnaissance and rail transport made the hunt through the mountains of northern Mexico a tedious failure. Villa remained uncaptured, although his forces were dispersed. *Below*, a detachment of U.S. Cavalry is seen on a scout.

Courtesy, Brown Brothers, New York City

Courtesy, Underwood-Stratton, New York City

In the picture *above*, some Villistas captured toward the end of April are under the large hats on the *right*—but not seen.

Preparedness

As the European belligerents continued to trespass on the rights of the United States and other neutrals, President Wilson became convinced that a greatly strengthened Army and Navy might give his protests more weight. He proposed a National Defense Act which became law in June, 1916.

Courtesy, Brown Brothers, New York City

While Congress debated the bill, "Preparedness Parades" took place in various localities. In New York City the paraders marched until far into the night of May 13, 1916. *Above*, a unit is seen passing the Public Library at 42nd Street and 5th Avenue.

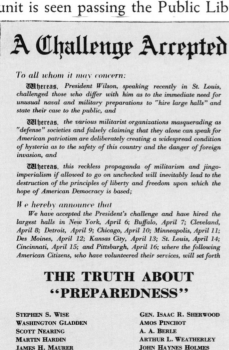

A Challenge Accepted

To all whom it may concern:

Whereas, President Wilson, speaking recently in St. Louis, challenged those who differ with him as to the immediate need for unusual naval and military preparations to "hire large halls" and state their case to the public, and

Whereas, the various militarist organizations masquerading as "defense" societies and falsely claiming that they alone can speak for American patriotism are deliberately creating a widespread condition of hysteria as to the safety of this country and the danger of foreign invasion, and

Whereas, this reckless propaganda of militarism and jingo-imperialism if allowed to go on unchecked will inevitably lead to the destruction of the principles of liberty and freedom upon which the hope of American Democracy is based;

We hereby announce that

We have accepted the President's challenge and have hired the largest halls in New York, April 6; Buffalo, April 7; Cleveland, April 8; Detroit, April 9; Chicago, April 10; Minneapolis, April 11; Des Moines, April 12; Kansas City, April 13; St. Louis, April 14; Cincinnati, April 15; and Pittsburgh, April 16; where the following American Citizens, who have volunteered their services, will set forth

THE TRUTH ABOUT "PREPAREDNESS"

STEPHEN S. WISE	GEN. ISAAC R. SHERWOOD
WASHINGTON GLADDEN	AMOS PINCHOT
SCOTT NEARING	A. A. BERLE
MARTIN HARDIN	ARTHUR L. WEATHERLEY
JAMES H. MAURER	JOHN HAYNES HOLMES
HERBERT BIGELOW	JOHN A. McSPARRAN

Signed: ANTI "PREPAREDNESS" COMMITTEE
Munsey Building, Washington, D. C.

There were those who did not agree with the President. William Jennings Bryan had already resigned as Secretary of State in protest against the policy of the United States. Now, in answer to the preparations for national defense, a group of citizens issued the broadside at the *left* and proposed to argue the matter.

Courtesy, The New-York Historical Society, New York City

The War Intrudes

For a few hours on the night of July 30, 1916, the thunder and red glare of the Western Front came to Jersey City, N. J., and the New York harbor area. German saboteurs exploded the munitions shipping station on Black Tom Island.

A number of persons were killed and as may be judged from the picture *above*, taken after the fire was checked, property damage was extensive.

On Aug. 23, 1916, the German submarine *Deutschland*, a cargo-carrier, ran the British blockade. She is shown *below* on her arrival at Baltimore, Md.

Both illustrations on this page are by the *courtesy* of Brown Brothers, New York City

Social Advance

Domestic reforms instituted by the Administration were less spectacular than the actions required of it by the war in Europe, but they were effective and solidly conceived. Idealism marked the politics of the day and the mood of American society began to conform.

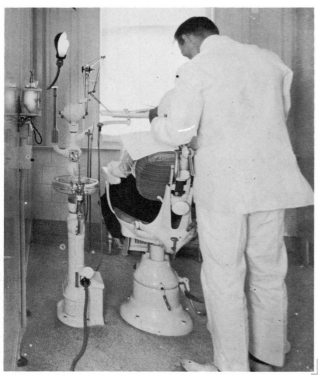

Courtesy, Metropolitan Life Insurance Co., New York City

Employee Relations

Enlightened corporations were voluntarily supplying services which helped to keep their staffs healthy and happy. At the *left* is seen part of the free dental clinic maintained by an insurance company.

"Be Prepared"

Many men were giving their time and skill to the work for betterment of American boys conducted by the Boy Scouts of America. This organization received its Federal charter in June, 1916, and the contemporary picture at the *right* shows a "time trial" in the practice of first aid to injured persons. This was one of many practical skills which scouting emphasized.

Courtesy, Boy Scouts of America, New York City

Emotion on the Screen

Varied fare was offered to the movie-goer of 1916. At the *right*, Roscoe ("Fatty") Arbuckle is seen in an episode of "Fatty at Coney," an early example of Arbuckle's subtle comedy technique.

William Fox reached deep down in the barrel for some of the vehicles in which Theda Bara (*below* at the left) appeared in 1916. Mrs. Wood's tearful "East Lynne" provided the scene *below*, a play which in the words of a critic "is perennially attractive to adolescents of all ages."

Both illustrations on this page are by the *courtesy* of Photoplay, New York City

Spectacles

Following on his success with "The Birth of a Nation," D. W. Griffith directed and produced "Intolerance" in 1916, another revelation of hidden possibilities in screen entertainment. One of the crowd scenes from "Intolerance" is shown *below*.

Courtesy, Film Library, The Museum of Modern Art, New York City

Town & Country, Sept. 1, 1916
Courtesy, Town & Country, New York City

On the Stage

At the *left*, the Dolly Sisters, Rozsika and Yancsi, are seen as they appeared at the final curtain of "His Bridal Night," a 1916 farce.

Broadway

For the tenth season of his "Follies," Flo Ziegfeld outdid himself in providing a show of sufficient gorgeousness and eye-appeal to match the occasion. His book-writers even rewrote a few Shakespearian scenes for inclusion among the Hula numbers and the tableaux.

Miss Allyn King (*right*) was chosen to be "The Follies Girl of 1916," and Miss Ann Pennington (*below*) made the best of the gifts with which nature had endowed her.

Town & Country, July 20, 1916
Courtesy, Town & Country, New York City

Town & Country, July 20, 1916
Courtesy, Town & Country, New York City

Actresses still struck on occasion the cigarette-premium poses of an earlier day. At the *right* is a publicity portrait of Eva Tanguay, whose raucous protest that she didn't care was heard from coast to coast.

"My voice, it may sound funny
But it brings me in the money—
And I don't care!"

Courtesy, Brown Brothers, New York City

Campaign of 1916

Woodrow Wilson had successfully begun a program of social reform, and he had "kept us out of war." There was no question about his renomination.

The President is shown *left* at Long Branch, N. J., as he listened to the official notice of his renomination, brought to him by Senator Ollie James of Kentucky in a speech before almost thirty thousand people.

Peace with Honor! 771536
Preparedness!
Prosperity!

THE
Democratic Text Book
1916

Copyright by HARRIS & EWING

Woodrow Wilson

Far and wide, the Democratic Party circulated its "Campaign Book" in which were stated reasons for the President's re-election. *Right* is shown a page from the book, and on its front cover (*left*) may be read the campaign slogans.

FIGURE IT YOURSELF— How Much Do We Owe Woodrow Wilson?

LAST JULY THE AMERICAN PEACE SOCIETY ESTIMATED THE TOTAL COST OF THE WAR AT THE END OF TWO YEARS AT MORE THAN $140,000,000,000, BASING ITS ESTIMATES ON THE CONSERVATIVE FIGURES OF SOME OF THE FOREMOST EUROPEAN STATISTICIANS, SUCH AS EDGAR CRAMMOND, OF ENGLAND; HENRI MASSON, OF BELGIUM; YVES GUYOT, OF FRANCE; MONSIEUR BARRIOL, OF RUSSIA; VON RENAULT AND RIESSER, OF GERMANY, AND THE AUSTRIAN MINISTER OF NATIONAL DEFENSE.

THIS HUGE COST INCLUDED DIRECT EXPENDITURES AND INDIRECT COSTS DUE TO LOSSES OF PROPERTY AND CAPITAL, AND WAS DIVIDED THUS:

GERMANY	$47,805,000,000
ENGLAND	27,350,000,000
FRANCE	22,025,000,000
AUSTRIA	23,790,000,000
RUSSIA	18,770,000,000
BELGIUM	5,540,000,000
ITALY	11,000,000,000

MINISTER GUYOT, OF FRANCE, HAS DECLARED THAT "THIS VAST DRAIN ON THE WORLD'S FINANCES IS CALCULATED TO PUT THREE-FOURTHS OF THE WORLD IN PAWN, WERE IT TO CONTINUE FOUR YEARS LONGER, LEAVING THE UNITED STATES AS THE ONLY SOLVENT NATION ON EARTH."

AND THIS REVEALS ONLY THE FINANCIAL SIDE OF THE "HELL" FROM WHICH WOODROW WILSON HAS SAVED THE UNITED STATES.

Campaign of 1916 (*Continued*)

The Republican Convention, June 10, 1916, chose Charles Evans Hughes to be Republican candidate for the Presidency, although Progressives had hoped for Theodore Roosevelt. The ex-President announced his support of the Republican ticket and his refusal to run again under the Bull Moose emblem, an action dictated by his fear and loathing of Wilson's policies. A reunited Republican Party stood a good chance of victory. The bearded nominee is seen *below* at center, speaking in August at Winona, Minnesota, from the observation platform of his campaign train.

Courtesy, United Press International Photo

The Republican rally *below* featured the candidate as speaker; it was held in New York City's Union Square on November 4, 1916.

Courtesy, Culver Pictures, Inc., New York City

11
END OF AN ERA

While the nominating conventions were in session and the rival candidates were maneuvering for position; while Frenchmen, Englishmen and Germans battled on the flat country around Bapaume and Peronne in the great Somme River offensive; the people of the United States enjoyed a peaceful summer, disturbed only by the war pictures in newspaper rotogravure supplements.

Thousands of city-bound people went to bathe in the surf at beaches like New York's Manhattan Beach (*above*). The Oriental Hotel may be seen in the background.

A "goose-chase" contest in Long Island Sound (*below*) attracted an audience from suburban Larchmont's Yacht Club.

Both illustrations on this page are by the *courtesy* of Underwood-Stratton, New York City

Summer Sport

Canoe races were popular at Moosehead Lake, Me. (*right*).

Courtesy, The Long Island Railroad, New York City

Courtesy, The Long Island Railroad, New York City

The morning hours were the traditional bathing hours at West Hampton, Long Island (*left*).

Hill Top Inn, on Bellevue Avenue, Newport, R. I., housed many prominent guests, and its Wednesday and Saturday tea dances were popular affairs. At the *right*, Rear Admiral H. T. Mayo and officers of his staff are seen outside the Inn.

The Spur, Aug. 15, 1916

Touring

Restless Americans who did not care for the local delights of the seashore betook themselves to the National Parks for change of environment.

Western coaches met the trains at the Gardiner, Mont., railroad station shown *above*.

The road up Mt. Washburn in Yellowstone Park (*below*) was best negotiated by a sure-footed team.

Both illustrations on this page are by the *courtesy* of the National Park Service

Sundays at Home

The baseball park was a pleasant place to spend the afternoon. The town boys were playing the team from the factory.

The picture *above* was taken near Pittsburgh, Pa.

In the evening, if it were not too hot, the local movie house was the place to go. There was a new comedy showing, "The Adventurer," with Charlie Chaplin and Edna Purviance.

Normal Things

The customary chores and small activities of the average American citizen were performed in a mood of personal security made all the more precious by what newspapers called "the European holocaust."

Courtesy, Mrs. Bert Gilmor, Los Angeles, Calif.

On a farm near Ada, Mich., the woman seen at the *left* experienced this sense of security, just as did the trolley passengers in Richmond, Va., *below*.

Courtesy, The Valentine Museum, Richmond, Va.

As Fall Came On

The old passenger whaleback *Christopher Columbus* (right) was still making the run between Chicago and Milwaukee.

Courtesy, St. Louis County Historical Society, Duluth, Minn.

Near Pittsburgh, Pa., workmen cycled to the factory in the pleasant warmth of Indian summer.

Courtesy, H. J. Heinz Company, Pittsburgh, Pa.

In the suburbs of Chicago, laundry was delivered in the handsome style illustrated at the *right*.

Courtesy, International Harvester Company, Chicago, Ill.

School Days

The pains of childhood were renewed as school reopened.

Courtesy, Public Roads Administration, Washington, D. C.

The picture *above* was taken in Lauderdale County, Ala. Two small boys enjoy the last moments of freedom.

As part of their education, North Carolina school children were set to picking cotton.

Courtesy, North Carolina State Department of Archives and History, Raleigh

Cabaret

The fall of 1916 saw customers thronging as never before to night resorts which offered a dance band and entertainment along with food and drink.

Courtesy, Brown Brothers, New York City

The scene *above* was photographed at the Cafe Beaux Arts, New York City.

Jazz

Afro-American rhythms for dancing, the "jazz" idiom, first came to be popular in the East as performed and recorded by the Original Dixieland Jazz Band. The band is shown *right* as it appeared at Reisenweber's Cafe, New York City.

Courtesy, Brown Brothers, New York City

Shall We Dance

It was a dancing time, very gay and light of heart.

Courtesy, Brown Brothers, New York City

Merrymakers, young and old, met at the "Cascades" ballroom of New York's Biltmore Hotel *above*. It was "smart" to go there. Note the waiter at the lower right.

Old and New

A third traditional ingredient went along with the dancing and the singing.

Family saloons like Rudolph Steinbacher's Milwaukee tavern shown *right* catered to one class of customer in 1916.

Bustanoby's New York City cafe had a different kind of trade. As proved *below*, Bustanoby's was up-to-date and tolerated women at its bar.

But it was later than they thought.

Courtesy, Wisconsin State Historical Society, Madison

Courtesy, Brown Brothers, New York City

Victories in Sight

The men and women who had fought for years against the liquor trade were heartened in their struggle as the spring of 1917 drew on.

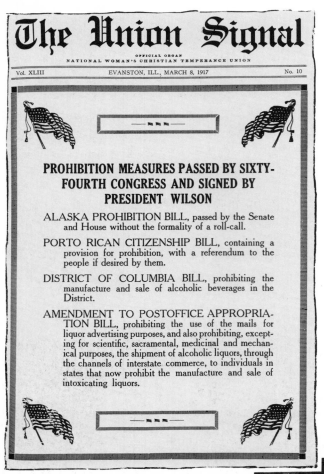

Courtesy, National Woman's Christian Temperance
Union, Evanston, Ill.

At the *left* appears a front cover from the official organ of the Woman's Christian Temperance Union.

"I wudden't be surprised at anny min-yit if I had to turn this emporyum into an exchange for women's wurruk," commented Mr. Dooley, the immortal saloon keeper of Archey Road.

Agitation had begun as well against cheap and often porno-graphic reading supplied to the young by mail.

The advertisement *right* stressed the positive side of this campaign.

Courtesy, N. W. Ayer & Son, Inc., Philadelphia, Pa.

Peace Without Victory

Charles Evan Hughes had gone to bed on election night, 1916, believing himself President. As returns continued to come in, his lead dwindled, and the electoral votes of California determined his defeat. Woodrow Wilson had been re-elected, by twenty-three electoral votes.

Assured of popular support, President Wilson redoubled his efforts to achieve a European peace without bitterness. His proposals failed to influence either set of belligerents. The German high command, driven to desperation by the throttling grip of the Allied blockade, forced the Reichstag to reopen unrestricted submarine warfare, despite promises made in answer to Wilson's earlier protests. After Feb. 1, 1917, German submarines were to sink on sight all vessels found in a clearly delimited zone around the British Isles and in the Mediterranean. One United States ship would be permitted a weekly call at the port of Falmouth, but she would have to bear distinctive markings and carry no contraband of war.

On Feb. 3, 1917, the President informed Congress that he had broken off diplomatic relations with Germany. Late in February, the State Department received evidence that Germany was acting to bring Mexico into the war against the United States should the diplomatic rupture lead to more serious action. While a Senate filibuster fought to prevent the arming of American merchant ships, several of them were torpedoed by German submarines. War had come in fact. Once again President Wilson appeared before Congress.

Courtesy, Underwood-Stratton, New York City

At 8:30 P.M., Apr. 2, 1917 (note clock in picture *above*), as a soft, spring rain fell over the Capitol, the President called for war. There was pandemonium in the crowded hall of the House of Representatives as he concluded ". . . the day has come when America is privileged to spend her blood and her might for the principles that gave her birth and happiness and the peace which she has treasured. God helping her, she can do no other."

Mobilization

Our new allies cried for ships, credit, shells, food. Our whole industrial and agricultural potential would have to be geared to war. The President delegated his extraordinary war powers to boards and commissions, which had sweeping authority over shipbuilding, the control of production and distribution, the floating of war loans and the seizure of essential facilities.

Attention!

ALL MALES between the ages of 21 and 30 years, both inclusive, must personally appear at the polling place in the Election District in which they reside, on

TUESDAY, JUNE 5th, 1917

between the hours of 7 A.M. and 9 P.M. and

Register

in accordance with the President's Proclamation.

Any male person, between these ages, who fails to register on June 5th, 1917, will be subject to imprisonment in jail or other penal institution for a term of one year.

NO EXCUSE FOR FAILURE TO REGISTER WILL BE ACCEPTED

NON-RESIDENTS must apply personally for registration, at the office of the County Clerk, at Kingston, N. Y., AT ONCE, in order that their registration cards may be in the hands of the Registration Board of their home district before June 5, 1917

Employers of males between these ages are earnestly requested to assist in the enforcement of the President's Proclamation.

Signed,

BOARD OF REGISTRATION
of Ulster County
E. T. SHULTIS, Sheriff
C. K. LOUGHRAN, County Clerk
Dr. FRANK JOHNSTON, Medical Officer

Meanwhile, under the Selective Service Act of May, 1917, civilian administrators set about raising an army. This was to be no war of volunteers. All men between twenty-one and thirty were obliged to register.

At the *left* is a draft poster as displayed in Ulster County, N. Y.

Despite gloomy predictions, the registration was orderly. In the picture *below* is a typical line-up in New York City, June 5, 1917.

Courtesy, The New York Historical Society, New York City

Courtesy, Brown Brothers, New York City

Industrial Mobilization

The War Shipping Board set about "bridging the Atlantic" with ships. Great new ship-yards were built and existing facilities like the Wilmington, N. C., yard at the *right* worked day and night. The schooner shown at the far right was tor-pedoed off the North Carolina coast early in 1918.

Courtesy, North Carolina State Department of Archives and History, Raleigh

Far under the earth, timbering operations like that shown *left* marked extension of copper mines, even though prices had been forced down from their 1916 peak.

The original hand-operated plate mill with which Andrew Carnegie had begun opera-tions at Upper Union Mills, Pittsburgh, Pa., was working at capacity to handle the 1917 demand for steel. (*Below*).

Courtesy, Anaconda Copper Mining Company, New York City

Courtesy, United States Steel Corporation, New York City

Transport

Efficient operation of domestic shipping systems was essential if the war were to be won.

Courtesy, Mr. Thomas B. Dancey, Dearborn, Mich., and Captain Fred A. Samuelson, Ludington, Mich.

Great Lakes traffic was a major artery. Car ferries are breaking through the ice off Ludington, Mich., in the picture *above*.

All American railroads were unified under Government operation in December, 1917. The 1917 locomotive shown *below* was working for Uncle Sam.

Courtesy, Chicago, Burlington & Quincy Railroad Company, Chicago, Ill.

Agriculture

In May and June, 1917, the prices of agricultural commodities soared. Extraordinary purchases had upset the normal balance of supply and demand. The United States Food Administration under Herbert Hoover took control and succeeded in stabilizing prices.

Courtesy, Great Northern Railway Company, St. Paul, Minn.

All was well on the Montana farm *above*. Wheat had risen to $3.25 a bushel before the Chicago Board of Trade stopped trading on May 11, 1917.

When the picture *below*, of cotton shipments from El Campo, Tex., was taken in the summer of 1917, cotton was selling at twenty-seven cents a pound, the highest price since Civil War days.

Courtesy, The Library of the University of Texas, Austin

Timber

Timber was driven down rivers to the sawmills, as in the view *left*, to meet the expanding quotas of the ship-building program.

Photo by United States Forest Service. *Courtesy*, Scribner Art File

In areas around booming warplants, lumber was needed urgently for housing. The 1917 picture *right* shows new homes for workmen at the mills in Lexington, N. C.

Courtesy, North Carolina State Department of Archives and History, Raleigh

Fish

Institution by the Food Administration of "Meatless Tuesdays" and "Porkless Thursdays" made fish an accepted item in the diet of the whole nation. At the *left*, a big one comes ashore at Warroad, Minn.

Courtesy, Minnesota Historical Society, St. Paul

Public Opinion

American public opinion was mobilized as well. The Committee of Public Information labored day and night to convince all American citizens that the war was both righteous and necessary.

Courtesy, U. S. Signal Corps, Washington, D. C.

In consequence, when the First Illinois Infantry marched out of its Chicago Armory to training camp (*above*) each man knew that he was dedicated to the righting of a grievous wrong.

The nation was one in spirit, as it was one in industrial and military effort. In October, 1917, the committee shown *below* met to receive back from Yankee hands a North Carolina flag taken at New Bern in 1862.

Courtesy, North Carolina State Department of Archives and History, Raleigh

Draftees

To the cheers and applause of their countrymen, the men of military age went off to war in 1917.

Parades of drafted men were common. *Above*, a group of draftees wait for their turn to swing into a march up Fifth Avenue, New York City.

Friends and relatives thronged down to Union Station to see the young men of Kansas City, Mo., depart for camp.

Both illustrations on this page are by the *courtesy* of the U. S. Signal Corps, Washington, D. C.

Soldiers

Draftees of 1917 made jokes (as Americans always do in serious moments) when they set off to learn the ways of war at Camp Kearney or McClellan or Devens, or at Camp Upton, Long Island, the destination of the New Yorkers *below*.

Courtesy, U. S. Signal Corps, Washington, D. C.

From men like these an army was made. After some six months' training and endless rumors, orders came. A tight-packed train to an embarkation camp! And then a jammed transport in convoy, protected by smoke screens and circling destroyers!

Courtesy, U. S. Navy Department, Washington, D. C.

Lafayette, We Are Here

Ignorant of war, high-spirited, idealistic, units of the American Army landed on French soil.

But after the run down a transport's gangway (*above*) there was another training period to undergo before active service at the front.

French and English officers returned from the advanced sectors to lend a hand in practice maneuvers on old battlefields.

Both illustrations on this page are by the *courtesy* of the U. S. Signal Corps, Washington, D. C.

Moving Up

Towards the end of 1917, only the First American Division had actively engaged the enemy. But seasoned troops had to be hurried across Europe to rescue the failing Italians—the Russians turned their guns on one another—and the defense of the Western Front was thrust suddenly on the men from Chicago and New York, from the little towns and the lonesome farms of America.

War has always been largely a matter of waiting. The French roads with their neat borders of trees were usually shrouded in rain. The picture *above* is a rarity.

When the trucks arrived at their destination, the real thing began—the sodden trenches, the stinks, barrages, patrols, raids—

Both illustrations on this page are by the *courtesy* of the U. S. Signal Corps, Washington, D. C.

Action

German divisions released by the Russian collapse were hurled against the Allied lines.

Amid the splintered trees of what had been a forest, the machine-gun company *above* crouched down and fought back. Infantrymen hugged the French earth while the ground ahead was prepared for their feet.

Into A New World

Courtesy, U. S. Signal Corps, Washington, D. C.

Up the slope and over the crest, by day or by night, against the machine gun's burst, the wire, the sniper's rifle, at Mondidier, Cantigny, Belleau Wood, the Second Marne, the American soldier was a symbol of his country's entry into a new world, a new set of responsibilities.